The Complete Guide to Compensation Planning with Life Insurance

LOUIS S. SHUNTICH, J.D., L.L.M.

MARKETPLACE BOOKS
COLUMBIA, MARYLAND

ISBN 1-59280-056-4

Printed in the United States of America.

This book is dedicated to my wife Suwannee.

Contents

Foreword

Dear Financial Service Professional:

A commitment to lifelong learning was one of the fundamental principles upon which the Society of Financial Service Professionals was founded back in 1928. While our industry, culture, and society have changed significantly in the intervening 75 years, this basic tenet has never wavered.

The Society's mission statement also highlights a commitment to continuing education that is current, comprehensive, and practical, and which extends the collective wisdom of our membership.

The Complete Guide to Compensation Planning with Life Insurance book is timely and concise. It includes an overview of the various compensation plans available, the many features each plan offers, and a summary of how they compare and can be applied to different scenarios. The compact, easy-reference format makes this guide both simple to follow and easy to use. In short—it's an ideal education tool for today's information-hungry and time-strapped professionals in their quest for learning.

This new guide can help you in your efforts to help your clients attract and retain high caliber employees in a competitive workplace.

The Society continues to distinguish itself among other financial service membership organizations with its requirement that members hold a recognized degree or credential, such as CLU, CFP, CPA, JD, ChFC, and CEBS. The Society endeavors to create a professional home for these credentialed individuals who share a belief in a core set of values—education, ethics, and relationships. As the professional home for our members, the Society provides a creative environment for professional growth which includes our Code of Professional Responsibility, access to networking opportunities, continuing education programs, and educational tools such as this new work by a recognized industry expert.

We hope this books helps to support your growth and learning in an important area of your professional life—and we wish you happy and fulfilling travels in your journey of professional learning.

Best regards,

Alan R. Ziegler, CEBS, CLU, ChFC
President, *Society of Financial Service Professionals*

The Complete Guide to Compensation Planning with Life Insurance

Introduction

Ask anyone who runs a business these days and they will tell you that a major factor in their success rests with their ability to attract the best people. In a highly competitive business arena, putting together the right compensation package can make the critical difference between getting - or losing - a key prospect. Highly paid individuals also need to find ways to mitigate their tax liabilities - so structuring the best compensation package possible becomes a primary factor in any salary negotiation. And - the financial advisors that dispense guidance to both sets of clients must be completely up-to-date on the various compensation plans and their tax implications, in order to advise their customers accordingly.

The catch is - busy professionals rarely have time to sift through all the information and paperwork on the many options available. For years, clients and associates alike have expressed the need and desire for a compact guide that would briefly but concisely list the various plans available, highlight the significant features of each, and provide an overview of how the compare and can be applied to different scenarios.

In *The Complete Guide to Compensation Planning with Life Insurance*, I've attempted to do just that. It's not an authoritative or exhaustive study of the material, and it doesn't try to be. Instead, I've attempted to fill an industry void by providing an efficient but not overwhelming reference source on the topic.

> I've attempted to fill an industry void by providing an efficient but not overwhelming reference source on the topic.

In the first few chapters I address the most common executive bonus plans, and some variations on them - highlighting the unique features of the plans, the pros and cons of each, related tax issues and basic ERISA concerns. In Chapter 3, we move into the realm of plans designed for government and non-profit entities. Chapters 5 through 7 deal with the applications of life insurance - including the goals of the various plans, funding options, tax implications and other important concepts. Chapter 8 addresses the Death Benefit and severance pay plans that were severely affected by recent changes in the tax codes. And in Chapter 9 I attempt to show how to compare and evaluate the various plans - and any new or unusual arrangements you may be interested in marketing in connection with life insurance.

> **The sweeping tax reforms of the 1990s had a big impact on the options highly compensated employees had to shelter their income.**

The sweeping tax reforms of the 1990s had a big impact on the options highly compensated employees had to shelter their income. Consequently - it had a big impact on the employers trying to structure plans that best served their employees, as well. It is my hope that this guide will help everyone involved in the process better understand - and apply - the information.

I also want to applaud organizations like the Society for Financial Professionals - who are dedicated to keeping industry professionals informed and educated on the changing regulations and issues we all face. Their commitment to continued learning and the support they provide keeps all affected professionals - from insurance agents, financial advisors and stockbrokers to lawyers and accountants informed - up-to-date and able to perform at the highest level of professional standards that we all aspire to.

Chapter 1

EXECUTIVE BONUS (SECTION 162) PLANS

Objective

The objective of this book is to provide an understanding of compensation arrangements that involve the use of life insurance either as a benefit or as the means of informally funding other benefits. This includes an explanation of IRC section 162 Bonus Plans, Restricted Bonus Plans, Nonqualified Deferred Compensation Plans, Split Dollar Life Insurance Arrangements, Group Term Carve Out Plans and Severance Pay Plans. The treatment of each of these subjects includes information on identifying prospects, the tax advantages and pitfalls to be avoided, the types of policies to be used and the circumstances under which each concept would most beneficially apply. Finally, guidance is provided on how to evaluate new or unusual compensation arrangements that you may be interested in marketing in connection with life insurance.

The Impact of Income Taxes on Compensation

> OBRA had a significant negative impact on highly compensated individuals by increasing their top income tax rate from 31% to 39.6%.

The 1993 tax act or OBRA had a significant negative impact on highly compensated individuals by increasingtheir top income tax rate from 31% to 39.6% and decreasing their itemized deductions and personal exemptions. The combined effect was to raise the top rate on such taxpayers to nearly 45%. Further, OBRA substantially decreased the amount of earnings upon which qualified pension benefits could be calculated.

The Economic Growth and Tax Relief Reconciliation Act of 2001 mitigates the effect of OBRA by reducing the top tax rate and phasing out the limitations on itemized deductions and personal exemptions. This relief is, however, only marginal and slow to happen. That is because the top rate drops as follows:

Calendar Year	39.6% Rate Reduced To
2001–2003	38.6%
2004–2005	37.6
2006–2007 and later	35.0

In addition, the phase out of the limitations on itemized deductions and personal exemptions is postponed so that they will be reduced by one-third in taxable years beginning in 2006–2007 and by two-thirds in taxable years beginning 2008–2009. Consequently, even after the 2001 tax act, the net effect of these developments is to still make tax favored benefit planning, for purposes of attracting and retaining key employees, crucially important for employers.

The Advantages of Life Insurance Oriented Compensation Arrangements

In marketing executive compensation arrangements that involve the use of life insurance, the initial question becomes: What advantages do they offer? That answer is twofold, with regard to the special tax treatment of policy benefits and the tax favored compensation arrangements with which they may be combined. Thus, there is a two-tiered or double tax benefit that stems from the products themselves and the transactions in which they are used. Further, these are nonqualified arrangements that have limited ERISA implications and this means that they may be selective as to who is covered and are not restricted as to the amount of benefits that may be provided.

> Thus, there is a two-tiered or double tax benefit that stems from the products themselves and the transactions in which they are used.

Design Features

Executive bonus plans (section 162) are the simplest and easiest of all executive benefit plans to establish and administer. This is because all the employer has to do is arrange for the executive to purchase a life insurance policy on which the employer will pay the premiums or give the executive a bonus with which to pay them. The executive is normally the applicant and owner of the policy and the only cost to the executive is the income tax that the executive pays on the employer's contribution. Even that may be offset, however, by having the employer pay a bonus to the executive of an additional amount to cover the tax. Further, since the executive owns the policy, he or she has access to its cash values that may be accessed for any reason, including paying taxes on the employer's premium contributions. The executive's ownership of the policy also makes the benefit completely portable. This means that the executive can leave the employer's service for any reason and keep the policy.

Plan Diagram

The following is a diagram of how the plan looks:

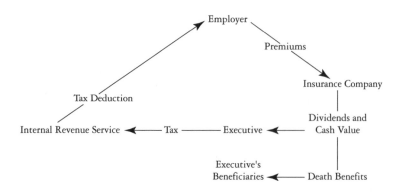

From the employer's perspective, there is complete discretion as to which executives are allowed to participate in the plan and how much insurance coverage they are provided. Normally, the plan covers key individuals and the amount of benefits matches their relative compensation level. As previously stated, these types of plans are the easiest to set up and run. The only disadvantage from the employer's side is the fact that each executive completely owns the policy on their life and that gives the employer no control over the asset. This lessens the effect of such plans, to act as "golden handcuffs" that bind valuable executives to the company.

> The most likely prospects for an executive bonus arrangement would be closely held small businesses with a few key people that the employer wants to retain or recruit.

Prospects for Executive Bonus Plans

The most likely prospects for an executive bonus arrangement would be closely held small businesses with a few key people that the employer wants to retain or recruit. In addition, the employer should consider the tax deductible nature of the premium payments a significant advantage.

Tax aspects.

The name "162 bonus plan" that is often used to describe these arrangements is derived from the fact that the employer's contributions, including any bonus to cover the executive's taxes, are deductible for income tax purposes under Internal Revenue Code (IRC) section 162 as an ordinary and necessary business expense. Conversely, the executive must include the employer's payments in income under IRC section 61. Further, the death benefits are income tax free under IRC section 101 but includible in the executive's gross estate under IRC section 2042 if the executive owns the policy or transfers it within three years of death. The estate tax exposure may be avoided if a third party such as a family member or an irrevocable trust is the applicant and owner of the policy from its inception.

ERISA concerns.

In those cases where the employer simply pays a bonus to purchase the policy, it is not clear that ERISA applies to the transaction. To the extent, however, that the arrangement may be characterized as a "welfare benefit plan" for ERISA purposes it would be subject to reporting and disclosure as well as fiduciary requirements. The reporting and disclosure requirements for a select group of executives are minimal but a summary plan description is required for larger groups. Further, for fiduciary purposes there must be a written plan instrument, with a named fiduciary and a claims procedure.

> The reporting and disclosure requirements for a select group of executives are minimal but a summary plan description is required for larger groups.

Suitable policies.

Any whole life insurance contract that fits the employee's personal or professional needs and objectives can be a suitable candidate. In that regard, if the employee is primarily concerned with financial security for their family, a traditional whole life contract is indicated. If, however, the employee's focus is on accumulating cash values for financial liquidity or supplemental sources of retirement funds, then contracts that are relatively more cash rich seem appropriate.

Illustration of Concept

The following is an illustrative example of how the concept works using figures drawn from an actual policy that are not for use with the public. Assume the executive is a nonsmoking 45-year-old in the 38.6% tax bracket and the employer is a corporation in the 35% tax bracket.

Year	Executive's Cumulative Bonus Income ($)	Employer's Cumulative After Tax Cost ($)	Executive's Cumulative Tax ($)	Cash Value ($)	Death Benefit ($)
1	15,625	10,156	6,031	0	501,769
2	31,250	20,312	12,062	753	501,769
3	46,875	30,468	18,093	10,463	503,775
4	62,500	40,624	24,124	21,180	506,287
5	78,125	50,780	30,155	32,365	509,325
6	93,750	60,936	36,186	44,106	512,849
7	109,375	71,092	42,217	56,420	517,047
8	125,000	81,248	48,248	70,269	521,905
9	140,625	91,404	54,279	84,716	528,367
10	156,250	101,560	60,310	99,761	535,509
15	234,375	152,340	90,465	188,668	585,187
20	312,500	203,120	120,620	311,213	672,475

Chapter 2

RESTRICTED BONUS ARRANGEMENTS

Design Features

This type of plan is a variation of the executive bonus plan described in Chapter 1 and, as the name implies, the arrangement places restrictions on the executive's ability to control the policy. The purpose of those limitations is to use the policy as a golden handcuff to keep the executive with the employer. That occurs through the executive and the employer entering into an agreement whereby the employer provides the funds to pay the premiums on the policy for as long as the executive is with the company or until the policy is paid up.

The executive is the owner of the policy but the ownership endorsement is modified to provide that the executive may not access or in any way encumber the cash value of the policy until a specified time or other triggering event without the employer's consent. For example, the restrictive endorsement may prohibit the executive from:

> The executive may not access or in any way encumber the cash value of the policy until a specified time or other triggering event without the employer's consent.

- Surrendering the policy

- Borrowing from the policy

- Taking cash withdraws

- Making a collateral or other assignment of the policy

- Changing the policy's ownership

With regard to triggering events that would cause a release of the restrictions on the executive's rights, typical provisions include:

- Retirement

- A fixed number of years

- Disability

- Death

- Termination without cause

Upon reaching the trigger, the employer's interest under the endorsement is removed and the executive acquires complete and unrestricted control of the policy and its benefits.

Plan Diagram

Here is a diagram of how the plan looks:

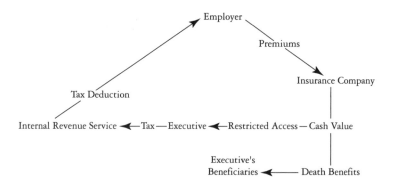

Prospects for Restricted Bonus Plans and Appropriate Policies

The prospects for these plans would essentially be the same as for section 162 bonus plans except that the employer would want to control the executives access to the policy's benefits as a form of stronger golden handcuff. Similarly, any policy that might be used for a 162 bonus plan would be appropriate for a restricted arrangement.

> Any policy that might be used for a 162 bonus plan would be appropriate for a restricted arrangement.

Tax Concerns

There is a substantial question as to whether the employer can take a current income tax deduction for its premium contributions under IRC section 162. This is because IRC section 264 prohibits a corporation from deducting premiums when it is a direct or indirect beneficiary of the policy. In that respect, the regulations under IRC section 264 show that the term "beneficiary" is broader than the mere right to receive death proceeds. Rather, it may extend to an economic interest in the policy of the type given to the employer under a restrictive endorsement. That interest is essentially the employer's power to force the executive to concede some portion of the cash value in return for the employer releasing its rights under the endorsement.

If IRC section 264 does apply, the employer's deduction under these plans would seem to be allowed at the time that the executive recognizes income under the arrangement in accordance with IRC section 83. In such case, income recognition under IRC section 83 occurs at the earlier of when the executive's rights become vested in the property or the property is transferable by the executive. That would not happen until the endorsement restriction is lifted at which time IRC section 83 states that the executive is taxed on the fair market value of the property. Consequently, since the IRS has held in two private letter rulings that the fair market value of a policy for purposes of IRC section 83 is its cash surrender value, that appears to be the amount that the executive would take into income and be the measure of the employer's deduction when the restriction is lifted.

Alternatively, if the employer's interest does not constitute that of a beneficiary for purposes of IRC section 264, the plan would be treated like a regular IRC section 162 bonus arrangement for tax purposes.

This means that the executive would recognize income on the premium payments as they are made and the employer would take its tax deductions at the same time.

Illustration of Concept

The following illustrations that are not to be used with the public, show the tax consequences of a restricted bonus arrangement under either approach to taxation. Assume that the executive is a 45-year-old nonsmoking male and the policy is a variable premium adjustable variable life. Note that the employer's bonus includes an additional amount to cover the employee's tax.

Bonus Currently Taxable to Executive and Deductible by Employer					
Year	Planed Insurance Payment ($)	Employer's Cumulative Bonus to Executive ($)	Employer's Cumulative After Tax Cost of Bonus ($)	Accessible Cash Surrender Value ($)	Death Benefit ($)
1	10,044	13,950	9,027	363	500,000
2	10,044	27,900	18,414	2,429	500,000
3	10,044	41,850	27,621	6,425	500,000
4	10,044	55,800	36,828	12,609	500,000
5	10,044	69,750	46,035	21,268	500,000
6	10,044	83,700	55,242	32,748	500,000
7	10,044	97,650	64,449	47,435	500,000
8	10,044	111,600	73,656	66,432	500,000
9	10,044	125,550	83,863	89,726	500,000
10	10,044	139,500	92,070	117,869	500,000
11	10,044	153,450	101,277	138,624	500,000
12	10,044	167,400	110,484	161,065	500,000
13	10,044	181,350	119,691	184,516	500,000
14	10,044	195,300	128,898	210,010	500,000
15	10,044	209,250	138,105	237,756	500,000

	Policy Cash Value Taxable to Executive and Deductible by Employer at Removal of Restrictions on Policy Endorsement				
Year	Planned Insurance Payment ($)	Cumulative Bonus to Executive ($)	Taxable Income to Executive ($)	Employer's Tax Deduction ($)	After Tax Cost to Employer ($)
1	10,044	13,950	0	0	
2	10,044	27,900	0	0	
3	10,044	41,850	0	0	
4	10,044	55,800	0	0	
5	10,044	69,750	0	0	
6	10,044	83,700	0	0	
7	10,044	97,650	0	0	
8	10,044	111,600	0	0	
9	10,044	125,550	0	0	
10	10,044	139,500	0	0	
11	10,044	153,450	0	0	
12	10,044	167,400	0	0	
13	10,044	181,350	0	0	
14	10,044	195,300	0	0	
15	10,044	209,250	237,756	237,756	126,335

ERISA Concerns

ERISA defines a pension plan as an employer established or maintained plan that either provides retirement income or results in the deferral of income by employees until the termination of employment or later. Consequently, to the extent that the restrictions on the endorsement lift at the termination of employment or at an age that could be considered retirement, the arrangement would seem to be a pension plan. Conversely, if the restriction were to lapse after a period of time that does not appear to be related to the executive's retirement, the arrangement would not seem to be a pension plan.

It would seem to be possible to draft a restricted bonus arrangement that did not constitute a pension plan by providing for the restriction to be lifted after a period of time or upon an event that did not coincide with the executive's termination of employment.

To the extent that a restricted arrangement is considered an ERISA pension plan, it would be subject to the reporting and disclosure rules, the fiduciary requirements, and the joint survivor annuity rules.

Chapter 3

PRIVATE SECTOR NONQUALIFIED DEFERRED COMPENSATION PLANS

Definitions

The term *nonqualified deferred compensation* has a broad meaning and is generally understood to cover the two following types of plans:

1. **Supplemental Executive Retirement Plans (SERP).** A type of plan that is established solely at the cost of the employer in that the employer agrees to pay the employee additional compensation in the future as a form of salary continuation.

2. **Traditional Deferred Compensation.** This type of arrangement involves a voluntary reduction in the employee's current income in return for the employer's promise to pay the funds with earnings thereon in the future.

Advantages of Supplemental Executive Retirement Plans (SERPs)

Due to the mandatory limitations on qualified retirement plan contributions and benefits, higher paid employees will typically receive a substantially smaller proportion of their income as a retirement benefit than their lower-paid counterparts. In that regard, nonqualified deferred compensation payments, in the form of SERPs, may be used to close this gap. In addition to increased retirement income, such plans

> Higher paid employees will typically receive a substantially smaller proportion of their income as a retirement benefit than their lower-paid counterparts.

offer the following advantages to highly paid employees:

- The recipients incur no taxes until the payments are received.

- These plans may include death and disability benefits.

- If the employee is in a lower tax bracket after retirement, more of the after tax benefit will be available than if the benefit had been paid before retirement.

- Employees, who take new positions too late in their careers to accumulate meaningful benefits under the new employer's qualified plan, can be given nonqualified SERP benefits to remedy the situation.

On the other hand, from the employer's perspective SERPS also offer the following advantages:

- The employer receives a tax deduction when the funds are paid to the employee.

- Benefits may vary among employees at the employer's discretion.

- The employer may choose which employees will participate without regard to the nondiscrimination rules that apply to qualified plans.

- IRS approval is not required to establish the plan.

- There are no statutory limitations on terminating the plan.

- These plans may be used to attract or retain valuable employees.

- These plans may be used as an alternative to giving employees an interest in the employer's business.

Advantages of Traditional Deferred Compensation Plans

These kinds of plans offer benefits that are similar to SERPs but an employee's willingness to enter into a traditional plan is typically affected by the employee's financial ability to forgo current income until a future time. Typical prospects for traditional deferred compensation plans are those executives who:

- Are looking to lower the taxes they are currently paying and are willing and able to reduce current salary and or bonus to achieve that objective.

- Want to accumulate capital for the long term.

- Need to put aside funds for disability protection and survivor benefits.

> An employee's willingness to enter into a traditional plan is typically affected by the employee's financial ability to forgo current income until a future time.

In any case, these plans may be combined with SERPs into a plan that involves employee deferrals and matching employer funds to get the benefit of both worlds.

Plan Diagram

Here is a diagram of what traditional deferred compensation plans and SERPs or a combination of both looks like:

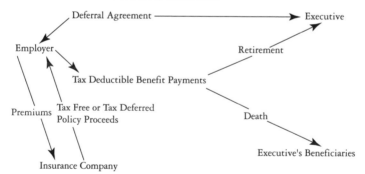

Establishing and Operating SERPS and Traditional Nonqualified Deferred Compensation Plans

SERPs and traditional deferred compensation plans are similar to establish and operate. Consequently, the following information applies to both types of plans with any differences pointed out where appropriate.

Corporate resolution.

When the employer is a corporation, a necessary step in the adoption of the plan is a resolution by the board of directors approving the establishment of the plan. Without such formal action to adopt, ratify, and record the plan, the agreement might be considered null and void under state law.

Use of life insurance.

An employer may use a whole life insurance policy as an informal funding vehicle to cover its liabilities to the employee or the employee's family. The arrangement is characterized as "informal" because the employee must not be given any interest in the policy or such an interest would destroy the tax deferral aspects of the plan. This means that the employer must be the applicant, owner, and beneficiary of the policy.

Advantages of informal funding with life insurance.

Because of its tax-favored treatment, life insurance has typically been the preferred asset for informally funding these plans. The income tax advantages of using life insurance include:

- Tax-deferred growth of policy cash values,

- Tax-favored access to cash values, and

- Tax-free death proceeds.

Further, life insurance policies are especially suited for matching the underlying asset to the employer's obligation to pay benefits. That is because such plans often provide preretirement disability and death benefits along with the postretirement income benefits. Considering that possible combination of benefits, generally no other asset can so readily parallel the employer's obligations and meet the timing of employer's need for funds.

Choice of Policy

There are a wide variety of policy types to choose from when informally funding a deferred compensation plan (traditional whole life, universal life, variable life, universal variable life, and joint life). Which particular type of policy will be best for a particular situation will depend on the facts and circumstances of the case and what the parties are trying to accomplish. Generally, however, where the goal is to create a large cash reserve, contracts that are more cash rich or investment oriented like variable policies are utilized. On the other hand, traditional whole life policies may also be attractive where they have competitive crediting rates and charges and are combined with substantial paid up additions. Term policies may even have application in those situations where the employer has a temporary cash flow problem and the plan provides death benefits to the employee's family. Recently, however, variable universal contracts have become particularly popular. This is especially true where the arrangement is structured as a defined

> The parties need to understand the risk associated with the uncertainty of any variable contract's performance.

contribution type of plan under which the employee's retirement benefits are measured by the performance of the policy. The parties need to understand the risk associated with the uncertainty of any variable contract's performance and its possible impact on the employee's benefits or the employer's ability to pay its obligations under the plan.

Paying Benefits

In using a life insurance policy to pay benefits, an employer enjoys the flexibility of several alternatives in choosing how to make payment. Those choices and the particular advantages of each are as follows:

- **Cash value approach.** This method utilizes the cash value of the policy to make payments in one of two ways. They are:

  Policy loans. The employer may take policy loans to make payments to the employee at the interest rate stated in the insurance contract. Usually, this rate will be more favorable than the regular market rate. Upon each policy anniversary the employer pays the interest on the loan until the policy is surrendered or the loan is paid off through the policy death benefit.

  Cash surrender. The alternative use of cash values is to pay benefits through a surrender of the policy. This approach does not, however, take full advantage of the previously mentioned tax leveraging aspect of life insurance since the employer forgoes tax free death proceeds for surrender proceeds that will be taxable to the extent they exceed the employer's cost basis for the policy. It should be noted that alternatives to surrendering the entire policy are to surrender paid up additions or make withdraws under the contract (assuming that the policy is of a type that permits withdraws). Under IRC section 72, such withdraws would first be a recovery of basis. Then, when basis is fully recovered, a switch to policy loans could be made with no income tax liability as long as the policy is not a modified endowment contract.

- *Cost recovery method.* Under this approach, the employer's focus is on cost recovery. Consequently, the employer is not concerned that the policy produces sufficient cash value to pay benefits. Rather, the emphasis is on purchasing an adequate face amount of insurance to allow the employer to recover (1) the amount of benefit payments to the employee, (2) the premiums paid to the insurer, and (3) the opportunity cost of the premiums, that is, what the employer could have earned on the premium dollars had they been invested elsewhere.

Note: Should the employee die before benefit payments are to commence under either the cash value or cost recovery methods, the death proceeds can be used to immediately pay benefits to the employee's family. Further, regarding disability benefits, the employer can informally fund the payments by adding a waiver of premium rider to the policy on the employee's life. This would relieve the employer of the burden of having to make premium payments if the employee becomes disabled. In addition, the employer can use the premium savings in combination with its tax deduction for benefit payments to pay a disability benefit that is even larger than the premium saved. For example, assuming a premium of $5,000 per year, a corporation in the 34% tax bracket could pay a disability benefit of $7,575 per year ($5,000 divided by .66). Alternatively, the employer could cover the cost of the benefits through the purchase of a disability income policy on the employee.

Alternative Minimum Tax

Since 1986, corporations purchasing life insurance must consider the possible application of the alternative minimum tax (AMT). This does not necessarily mean that the ownership of the insurance will cause a minimum tax liability. Rather, the insurance cash values and death proceeds are only among many elements in determining whether the corporation will incur the liability. In addition, even when there is a liability, the effect is to tax cash value increases and death proceeds at only a 15% rate. Further, the amount of the annual cash value increases may be reduced by the premium cost of the coverage and death proceeds should be offset by cash value previously included in the calculation. Finally, if the corporation pays an AMT liability in one year, that amount will be available as a credit against regular tax liability in future years in which there is no AMT. Note that the Taxpayers Relief Act of 1997 exempts small corporations that meet a gross receipts test from the tax.

> Even when there is a liability, the effect is to tax cash value increases and death proceeds at only a 15% rate.

Accumulated Earnings Tax

This tax is imposed when the earnings of a corporation are accumulated beyond the reasonable needs of the business. The purpose of the tax is to prevent corporations from being used as a repository to shelter income from taxation in the hands of shareholders. In regard to accumulating income for the purpose of informally funding deferred compensation benefits owed to a minority shareholder employee, the Tax court held that such an accumulation was a reasonable business need. *John P. Scripts Newspapers v. Comm,* 44 TC No. 41 (1965). Similarly, an accumulation for the purpose of informally funding such benefits for a majority shareholder was also deemed reasonable in the case of *Oklahoma Press Publishing v. U.S.,* 437 F. 2d 1275 (10 Cir. 1971); on remand, 28 AFTR 2d 71-5722 (E.D. OK 1971). In any case IRC section 535(c)(2) allows earnings of up to $250,000 ($150,000 for a personal services corporation) to accumulate without question.

Modified Endowment Contracts

Pursuant to the Technical and Miscellaneous Revenue Act of 1988, the cash value of a life insurance contract may not be borrowed or withdrawn tax free if the contract is characterized a "modified endowment contract." These contracts are defined as life insurance contracts entered into after June 21, 1988 and which have a premium amount higher than that permitted under the "7 pay test" of IRC section 7702A. Under such a policy any loan or withdraw will be taxed to the extent that there is gain in the contract. There is gain in the contract when the cash value exceeds the net investment (premiums less any untaxed amounts previously received). In addition, there is a 10% penalty tax on the amount of any taxable gain incurred. What this means is that a modified endowment contract or MEC is not a suitable vehicle for informally funding a nonqualified deferred compensation plans. The reason is that withdraws or loans from such a policy to pay benefits will be subject to tax, including the extra 10% tax.

> There is gain in the contract when the cash value exceeds the net investment.

Inapplicability of Annuities

Since the Tax Reform Act of 1986, annuities owned by nonnatural persons such as corporations or trusts no longer enjoy tax deferred status for amounts invested in the annuity. This means that if, an annuity is purchased by a corporation to informally fund a deferred compensation plan, the employer will recognize taxable income on the contract between the time of purchase and the commencement of payments under the contract. Consequently, annuities should be avoided as an asset for informally funding deferred compensation plans.

The Doctrines of "Constructive Receipt" and "Economic Benefit"

The crucial issue to an employee under an informally funded deferred compensation plan is the timing of the recognition of income. If the plan is properly structured that will not occur until the employee receives the income. In this respect, care must be taken to avoid the employee becoming subject to the income tax doctrines of constructive receipt and economic benefit. This is because the employee will be taxed currently on amounts that the employee is deemed to have constructively received or enjoyed the economic benefit there from. Such a result can be disastrous for the employee since the employee would incur a tax liability without receiving the cash with which to pay the related tax. These important doctrines may be explained as follows:

- **Constructive receipt.** Pursuant to Treas. Reg. Section 1.451 an employee is deemed taxable on the income that is available to the employee or that the employee could have taken but chose not to. In addition, to assure the deferral of taxation until the desired tax period the employee's rights to the income must be subject to "substantial limitations or restrictions." Essentially, this means that the employee can have no right to receive the income until the proscribed event for payment under the agreement. For example, the employee should not be given any rights under the agreement that would permit the employee to accelerate the time for payment or allow the employee to assign the right to payment to a third party in satisfaction of a debt.

- **Economic benefit.** An employee cannot be taxed currently on the mere unsecured promise of an employer to pay a salary continuation benefit. Such a promise is not deemed to be susceptible of valuation. If, however, the employee is given an interest in an asset that was issued to fund the deferred compensation payments, that security interest will make the employee's right to payment susceptible of valuation and the employee will be treated as having received an economic benefit and will be subject to current taxation.

> An employee cannot be taxed currently on the mere unsecured promise of an employer to pay a salary continuation benefit.

IRS Requirements for a Favorable Private Letter Ruling

In two IRS announcements called *Revenue Procedures,* the Service has laid out the conditions for receiving a favorable Private Letter Ruling on a traditional salary reduction deferred compensation plan (Rev. Proc. 71-19, 1971-1 CB 698 and Rev. Proc. 92-65, 1992-2CB 428). This means that the IRS would approve of a salary reduction plan that meets the following conditions:

- The election to defer compensation must be made before the beginning of the taxable year for which the compensation is payable; provided, however, that in the year in which the plan is first implemented or the year in which a participant becomes first eligible to participate, such election may be made within 30 days after the plan is effective or the employee becomes eligible.

- The plan must define the time and method for payment of deferred compensation for each event (such as termination of employment, disability or death).

- The plan may provide for payment of benefits in the case of an "unforeseeable emergency." Unforeseeable emergency must be defined in the plan as an unanticipated emergency that is caused by an event beyond the control of the participant or beneficiary and that would result in severe financial hardship to the individual if early withdraw were not permitted. The plan must further provide that any early withdraw is limited to the amount needed to meet the emergency.

- The plan must provide that the participants have the status of general unsecured creditors of the employer and that the plan constitutes a mere promise by the employer to make payments in the future.

- If a trust is used, the trust must conform to the terms of the model Rabbi Trust described in Rev. Proc. 92-64 (described below).

- The plan must provide that a participant's rights to benefit payments under the plan are not subject in any manner to anticipation, alienation, sale, transfer, assignment, pledge, encumbrance, attachment, or garnishment by creditors or the participant or the participant's beneficiary.

- The IRS also requires that if the participant is permitted to make a change of election as to when payments are to be made, the participant's rights to the payments must be forfeitable to avoid current taxation of the funds as they are earned. Nonetheless, the IRS has lost in several court cases where the employer and employee agreed to further extend the time of payment after the deferred compensation agreement was entered into. See *Martin v. Commissioner,* 96 TC 814 (1991); *Oates v. Commissioner,* 18 TC 570 (1952), acq. 1960-1 CB 5, aff'd 207 F2d 711 (7Cir. 1953); *Viet v. Commissioner* 8 TC 809 (1947) acq. 1947-2 CB 4; *Viet v. Commissioner,* 8TCM 919 (1949).

Income Tax Consequences of Benefit Payments

The benefits are taxed to the employee in the year that they are actually received by the employee. See IRC section 451(a); Treas. Reg. Section 1.451(a); Rev. Rul. 60-31, 1960-1 CB 174. Similarly, the employer is entitled to an income tax deduction in the year that the employee takes the amount received into income. See IRC section 404(a) (5). Note, however, that the employer is not entitled to an income tax deduction for the premium payments on a policy purchased by the employer to informally fund the deferred compensation benefits. See IRC 264(a) (1).

> The employer is entitled to an income tax deduction in the year that the employee takes the amount received into income.

Payments to the employee's surviving beneficiary are income in respect of a decedent. Consequently, such amounts are subject to income tax when received by the beneficiary. The beneficiary is, however, entitled to an income tax deduction for any estate taxes attributable to the inclusion of the deferred compensation benefits in deceased employee's gross estate. See IRC section 691(c).

Estate Tax Consequences to the Employee

The present value of any benefit that is payable to a beneficiary will be includible in the employee's gross estate. See IRC sections 2036-2039. Note that in community property jurisdictions, amounts accrued during marriage will be community property. This means that if the non-employee spouse dies, a part of the present value of the benefit will be included in that spouse's gross estate. The problem is that this amount probably will not qualify for the estate tax marital deduction because the funds are not available.

Illustration of Concept

The following is an illustration of a SERP. It reflects an actual policy but is not to be used with the public. The policy is a flexible premium

Year	Annual Premium ($)	Policy Surrender ($)	Policy Loan ($)	Net Asset Value ($)	Annual Retirement Benefits ($)	Total Net Death Benefit ($)
1	5,000	0	0	3,661	0	253,661
2	5,000	0	0	7,623	0	257,623
3	5,000	0	0	11,916	0	261,916
4	5,000	0	0	16,576	0	266,576
5	5,000	0	0	21,635	0	271,635
6	5,000	0	0	27,135	0	277,135
7	5,000	0	0	33,118	0	283,118
8	5,000	0	0	39,629	0	289,629
9	5,000	0	0	46,722	0	296,722
10	5,000	0	0	54,466	0	304,466
11	5,000	0	0	63,425	0	313,425
12	5,000	0	0	73,154	0	323,154
13	5,000	0	0	83,622	0	333,622
14	5,000	0	0	94,892	0	344,892
15	5,000	0	0	107,025	0	357,025
16	5,000	0	0	120,129	0	370,129
17	5,000	0	0	134,245	0	384,245
18	5,000	0	0	149,452	0	399,452
19	5,000	0	0	165,836	0	415,836
20	0	14,718	0	162,263	13,034	401,094
21	0	14,718	0	158,426	13,034	386,351
22	0	14,718	0	154,145	13,034	371,608
23	0	14,718	0	149,347	13,034	356,865
24	0	14,718	0	143,979	13,034	342,122
25	0	14,718	0	137,980	13,134	327,379
26	0	6,693	8,025	131,295	13,134	312,315
27	0	0	14,718	123,297	13,134	296,675
28	0	0	14,718	115,704	13,134	280,409
29	0	0	14,718	106,642	13,134	263,493
30	0	0	14,718	96,626	13,134	245,898
31	0	0	14,718	85,564	13,134	227,601
32	0	0	14,718	73,352	13,134	208,572
33	0	0	14,718	59,860	13,134	188,782
34	0	0	14,718	44,968	13,134	168,200
35	0	0	0	44,562	0	162,102
Total					$195,508	

adjustable variable life on a male age 46 who is a nonsmoker. Assume that the initial specified amount is $250,000 and the initial premium is $5,000. Further, assume that the death benefit and cash values are illustrated based on a 9.15% illustrative net interest assumption and the employer is in the 34% tax bracket. (See table on page 32.)

Employees Retirement Income Security Act (ERISA)

Informally funded deferred compensation plans that are primarily for a select group of management or highly compensated employees (referred to as "Top Hat" plans) are exempt from the participation, vesting, and funding provisions of ERISA. See ERISA sections 201(2); 301(a) (3); 401(a) (1). If, however, the arrangement includes rank and file employees it will be subject to the participation, vesting, and funding rules.

Meaning of "unfunded."

From a labor law perspective, the Department of Labor seems to take the same position as the IRS in defining the meaning of "unfunded," that is, a plan is unfunded if it provides benefits solely from the general assets of the employer. See 29 CFR section 2520.104-23 (1988). Further, the Department of Labor issued Advisory Opinion 81-11A which provided that a deferred compensation plan that was informally funded with life insurance policicies was unfunded for ERISA purposes where the following conditions were met:

- The employer was the named beneficiary of the policies.

- The employer owned the policies and they were subject to the claims of the employer's creditors.

- Neither the plan nor any participating employee or beneficiaries had any preferred claims against the policies and they had no beneficial ownership interest in the policies.

- No representations were made to any participating employees or their beneficiaries that the policies would be used exclusively to provide benefits or were security for the payment of benefits.

- Plan benefits were not limited or governed in any way by the amount of insurance held by the employer.

- Participating employees were not required or permitted to contribute to the plan.

Meaning of "select group of management or highly compensated."

ERISA does not define this term but the following court cases offer some guidance:

- *Belka v. Rowe Furniture Corp.*, 571 F Supp. 1249 (DMD 1983). In this case, the court found that between 1.6% and 4.6% of the employees were covered by the plan and concluded that the plan qualified as a top hat plan.

- *Duggan v. Hobbs*, 99 F3d 307 (9th Cir. 1996). The court concluded that a plan that covered only one of twenty-three employees was a top hat plan.

- *Loffland Brother Co. v. Overstreet*, 758 P 2d 813 (Okl. S. Ct. 1988). The court found that there was a top hat plan where only 40 out of 4500 employees were covered by the plan.

- *Demery v. Extebrook Deferred Compensation Plan (B)*, F.3rd (2d Cir. 6/5/00) held that 15% of the employees was a select group but indicated that this was probably the upper limit.

- *Carrabba v. Randalls Food markets, Inc.*, 252 F.3rd 721 (5th Cir. 2001). In this case, the court determined that since all the management employees of the company were eligible to participate in the plan, it was not for the benefit of a "select group" of management employees. Consequently, the plan was found to not qualify for top hat treatment.

> For the exception to apply, the participants may be a select group of management or highly compensated employees.

The Department of Labor (DOL) has not issued regulations defining the meaning of the term "top hat plan," but it has indicated that such a group consists of those employees who have the ability to affect or substantially influence the design and operation of the plan. See DOL Advisory Opinion 90-14A (May 8, 1990). Note that for the exception to apply, the participants may be a select group of management or highly compensated employees.

Reporting and disclosure.

Unfunded top hat plans are subject to the reporting and disclosure requirements of ERISA. See CFR section 2520.104-23 (1988). However, a simplified alternative method of compliance has been established for such plans. The alternative approach permits the reporting and disclosure rules to be satisfied by filing with the Secretary of Labor a general statement about the plan including:

- The name and address of the employer.

- The employer's identification number assigned by the IRS.

- A statement that the plan is maintained primarily for a select group of management or highly compensated employees and the number of employees covered.

- The employer is required to provide documents to the DOL if requested.

Claims procedure.

ERISA section 503 may require a claims procedure for the participants and beneficiaries of unfunded top hat plans. Essentially, if a claim for benefits were denied, such a procedure would require a notice of the decision to the participant within a reasonable period of time. Further, the notice would have to give the specific reason for the denial and any additional information needed to perfect the claim. See 29CFR section 2560.503-1(f).

FICA taxes.

Amounts deferred are subject to the FICA wage base the later of (1) when the services are performed or (2) when there is no substantial risk of forfeiture. See 29CFR section 3121(v) (2) (A). This means that if the deferred amounts are not forfeitable, they are subject to FICA tax in the

> If the deferred amounts are not forfeitable, they are subject to FICA tax in the year the services are performed.

year the services are performed. If the benefits are forfeitable, the FICA tax will be due when the risk of forfeiture ceases. For example, if the benefits are forfeitable should the employee terminate before retirement at age 65, they will become nonforfeitable and subject to tax upon the employee's retirement at age 65. It should be noted that no FICA tax is due on the OASID component if the participant's other compensation for that year already exceeds the applicable wage base. There will, however, continue to be a 1.45% Medicare tax since the Medicare rate applies without regard to the amount of wages. Further, under final Treasury regulations that became effective on December 31, 1999, once amounts are deferred, only "reasonable" interest rates can be credited to those deferrals. If the rate of interest is not reasonable, then the excess interest is treated as an additional amount of compensation and is taxable for FICA purposes at the point of deferral. Further, the earnings on excess interest would be subject to FICA tax in the future. (The reasonable earnings on the original deferred amounts would not be subject to FICA tax.) See Treas. Regs. sections 31.3306(r) (2)-1 31.3121(v) (2)-1and 2.

Securing the Employer's Promise

The risk to the employee of deferring compensation is that the employer's circumstances may change and the employee might not be paid the promised benefits. That risk falls into the three following categories:

1. **Cash flow problems.** The employer may not be insolvent but lacks the cash to meet the payment obligations as they arise. This could string out the payment of benefits and disrupt the employee's financial plans that depend on timely payment.

2. **Change of control.** Management turnover could result in a change of attitude toward paying the benefits. The employee could sue the employer, but that would cost time and money that the employee may not have to spare.

3. **Insolvency.** If the employer goes bankrupt, the employee will have the standing of a mere unsecured creditor. That means that the secured

creditors will be paid ahead of the employee who may get little or nothing of the promised benefits.

Rabbi Trust

To deal with the two potential risks that the employee might not get paid because of cash flow problems or a change in management, the employer could establish a *Rabbi Trust* to hold the life insurance policy for the employee's benefit. The employer can create such a trust, in accordance with IRS Rev. Proc. 92-64, 1992-2 CB 422, without causing the deferred compensation benefits to be immediately taxed to the employee. While such a trust solves the financial risks associated with cash flow and a change of management, it does not eliminate the risk of nonpayment stemming from the employer's bankruptcy. The terms of IRS Rev. Proc. 92-65 require that the property in the trust be subject to the claims of the employer's creditors. As a result, the Rabbi Trust is a partial but not perfect solution to the risk of nonpayment of the deferred compensation benefits.

> The Rabbi Trust is a partial but not perfect solution to the risk of nonpayment of the deferred compensation benefits.

From a tax perspective, the employer does not get a tax deduction until the benefits are paid from the trust to the employee pursuant to IRC section 404(a) (5). Further, since the employer is treated as the owner of the trust, it must recognize all of the income of the trust on its tax return. Normally, that would not be a problem if the only asset of the trust is a life insurance policy since there is no tax on the growth of cash values left in the contract. There would be an exposure to taxation, however, to the extent that cash values are accessed by the employer to pay benefits or for other reasons.

Secular Trust

One way of eliminating even the risk associated with the employer's bankruptcy is for the employee to establish a *Secular Trust* to hold the funding asset for his or her own benefit. Such a trust is not subject to the claims of the employer's creditors. The price, however, that the employee has to pay for this form of security is that the assets that are placed into the trust will be currently taxed to the employee, even though the deferred compensation benefits are not payable until the future. That is because under IRC section 83 an employee is immediately taxed on property placed in such a trust. Worse yet, the IRS takes the position that highly compensated employees are taxed under IRC section 402(b) on their vested accrued benefit in the trust at the end of each year. This means that even the growth in the policy's otherwise nontaxable cash value may be taxed to the employee each year. These trusts were popular when corporate tax rates were higher than the individual rates because placing the assets in the trust accelerated the employer's tax deduction. Since the individual rates are now higher than the corporate rates, such arrangements have lost much of their appeal. It should be noted that where secular trusts are used the employer is likely to want to be the party that establishes the trust. This is because the employer will want to assure that the funds go into the trust for retirement needs and are not spent by the employee currently as might occur if the employee is given the funds to place in the trust. Pursuant to newly proposed regulations under 1.671-1(g), the IRS is of the view that only the employee can establish the trust and the employer cannot be treated as the owner for income tax purposes.

> The IRS takes the position that highly compensated employees are taxed under IRC section 402(b) on their vested accrued benefit in the trust.

Third-Party Guarantees

An alternative security arrangement is for the employer to obtain a third-party guarantee that the benefits will be paid to the employee. The problems with this approach are that this type of protection may be hard to find and the employee must be the party to pay the cost of the protection. If the employer bears the cost, the arrangement might be characterized by the IRS as a funded plan that would result in immediate taxation of the deferred benefits to the employee.

Deferred Compensation Triggers

It has been suggested that a Rabbi Trust may be drafted in which amounts that are payable to executives are automatically paid out on certain triggering events such as a drop in the net worth, a decline in credit rating, or other events tied to the insolvency of the employer. The Internal Revenue Service has, however, informally repeated its warning that it considers such plans to probably result in taxation to the employee when they are established because the triggering event precludes the employer's creditors from reaching the funds and the rights of such creditors are thereby defeated.

Stockholder Employees

To be deductible as an ordinary and necessary business expense under IRC section 162(a) payment of deferred compensation must be reasonable and not a disguised dividend. The difference being that while both are taxable income to the employee shareholder, compensation is deductible by the corporation but dividends are not. Regarding minority shareholder employees, there is usually no question that the payments are deductible as arm's-length negotiated compensation. Where a majority shareholder is

> The test of reasonableness of compensation does apply to a majority shareholder.

involved, the IRS has refused to rule on the issue (Rev. Proc. 93-3, 1993-1, CB 370) but indicated a belief that the individual's control over the entity constitutes constructive receipt of any deferred funds. The Tax Court seems, however, to take the view that the test of reasonableness of compensation does apply to a majority shareholder. The determination is to be made in consideration of compensation for the current year plus all prior years in light of all services rendered to the corporation by the individual up to the current year. See *Andrews Distributing Co. Inc. v. Commissioner,* 31 YCM (CCH) 732 41 TCM (P-H) 764 (1972).

Subchapter S Corporations

A Subchapter
S corporation
(S corporation) pays
no income tax.

Unlike a regular corporation, a Subchapter S corporation (S corporation) pays no income tax. Rather the S corporation's net income is taxed to the shareholders individually in proportion to their stockholding whether the income is distributed or not. Consequently, the shareholders of an S corporation cannot defer compensation.

SEC Registration Requirements

Generally to offer a security for sale the party must first register it with the SEC or qualify the offering for one of the several exemptions from the registration requirements. Based on the U.S. Supreme Court's decision in *International Brotherhood of Teamsters v. Daniel,* 99 S. Ct. 790 (1979) a involuntary and noncontributory nonqualified deferred compensation plan would not constitute a security, and therefore, not require registration. Prior to 1994 the SEC in a number of "no action" letters viewed voluntary contribution plans as qualifying for the "private offering" exemption to the registration requirements because they were typically seen as only applying to a relatively few top level executives. That perception changed, however, as the SEC became aware that some plans extended to rank and file employees and reflected returns based on market-oriented investments such as mutual funds or presumably variable life insurance policies. Focusing on this latter point, the SEC currently takes the position that contributory nonqualified deferred compensation plans may require registration where the employees' motivation for participation is investment oriented rather than merely an income tax saving. This is especially true where the plan involves investments in underlying securities whose rate of return is credited to the employees.

The SEC currently
takes the position
that contributory
nonqualified deferred
compensation plans
may require
registration.

In light of such a difficult facts and circumstances test, for determining whether to register a plan, employers seem to have three choices:

1. **Register the plan.** For a publicly traded company, a Form S-8 may be used which is usually not very burdensome or expensive. For a nonpublic company the requirements are substantially more onerous.

2. **Seek qualification for one of the exemptions from registration.**

   Nonpublic companies may offer up to $5 million a year (or 15% of the issuer's assets, if less) of unregistered interests to employees.

   A private offering exemption is also available where the participating employees are deemed to be "accredited investors" meeting certain net worth and income tests or have the knowledge and experience to evaluate the plan.

3. **Do nothing pending further guidance from the SEC.**

Generally, absent a showing of fraud, the penalty for failure to register seems to be that the participants can rescind their deferrals and seek a return of their investments with any loss falling on the employer. Some companies are registering their contributory plans while others are not, pending clearer guidance from the SEC. The bottom line is that the best advice seems to be for interested employers to talk to their own securities counsel before making a decision on these issues.

> The best advice seems to be for interested employers to talk to their own securities counsel.

Chapter 4

GOVERNMENT AND NONPROFIT IRC SECTION 457 PLANS

Background

In 1978, the IRS became concerned that state and local governments were not adopting qualified pension plans for their employees and were instead creating nonqualified salary reduction (traditional) deferred compensation plans in their place. The reason that the state and local governments were utilizing nonqualified plans in place of qualified plans was that, as nontaxable entities, they were not attracted by the tax deductions that prompt private sector employers to incur the additional expense and complexity associated with qualified pension plans. This meant that state and local government employees were not getting the protection of ERISA's vesting, funding, and participation rules.

To stop this trend, the IRS issued Reg. 1.61-19, which prohibited state and local governments from adopting salary reduction deferred compensation plans by denying participating employees the ability to defer taxes on the amounts that were set aside. In response, the state and local governments were able to get Congress to enact IRC section 457. That provision permits state and local governments to create nonqualified deferred compensation plans of two types, which are characterized as either "eligible" or "ineligible" plans.

Under IRC section 457(b) eligible plans, if the requirements described next are met, the participating employees of state and local governments are permitted to defer income taxes on the amounts that are set aside until those amounts are paid to the employees. This is true even though the employees' rights to the deferred amounts are vested at the time the deferrals are made. Conversely, if the requirements for eligibility are not met, the plan is referred to as an ineligible "457(f) plan" and the employees will be taxed on the deferrals at the time they are made, unless the employees' rights to the payments are subject to a substantial risk of forfeiture. Generally, a substantial risk of forfeiture is deemed to exist when the participant's rights to payment are conditioned upon the performance of substantial future services for the plan sponsor.

> State and local governments may establish unfunded IRC section 415(m) (3) "excess benefit plans."

State and local governments may establish unfunded IRC section 415(m) (3) "excess benefit plans" that only provide benefits in excess of the limitations imposed by IRC section 415 on qualified pension plans and are not subject to the deferred compensation limits of IRC section 457. Further, bona fide vacation leave, sick leave, compensatory time, severance pay, disability pay, death benefit plans, and plans that only pay length-of-service awards to volunteers are not covered by IRC section 457. Finally, IRC section 457 does not apply to church plans or qualified state judicial plans. The exception for church plans includes the plans of church-controlled organizations and qualified state judicial plans include any retirement plan of a state for the benefit of judges or their beneficiaries.

Plans of Tax-Exempt Organizations

As originally enacted, it was not clear whether IRC section 457 applied to nongovernmental organizations that are tax exempt under IRC section 501. That oversight was corrected, however, and generally for taxable years after December 31, 1986, section 457 applies to the deferred compensation agreements of such organizations. Nongovernmental tax-exempt employers must structure their plans to take advantage of an ERISA exemption or their plans will be subject to the funding requirements of ERISA. The most typical way of avoiding those requirements is to restrict participation to a select group of management or highly compensated employees (top hat plan) or structure the plan as an unfunded excess benefit plan. This means that for practical purposes, nongovernmental tax-exempt employers are limited to providing 457 plans to their top-level people.

Proposed Regulations

The IRS released proposed regulations on May 8, 2002, to update the regulations to IRC section 457. (See 67 Fed. Reg. 30826.) Those proposed regulations would generally be effective for taxable years after December 31, 2001, and make numerous additions and changes to the present rules including those mentioned in the following explanation of IRC section 457 plans.

IRC Section 457(b) Eligible Plan Requirements

Participation.

The IRC section 457(b) plan must limit participation to those who provide services to a state (this includes political subdivisions, agencies, or instrumentalities) or a tax-exempt organization as either an employee or independent contractor.

Timing of deferrals.

The proposed regulations state that the agreement to defer is valid if it is made before the first day of the month in which the compensation is paid or made available. Generally, this means that there is no requirement that the agreement be in effect before the services giving rise to the compensation are performed. On the other hand, compensation payable in the first month of employment may be deferred only if an agreement is entered into prior to the time a participant performs services for the employer.

> The agreement to defer is valid if it is made before the first day of the month in which the compensation is paid or made available.

Amount of deferrals.

Prior to the 2001 Tax Act, participants in an eligible plan were limited to deferring not more that 33⅓% of "includible compensation" or $7,500 as indexed for inflation. (The inflation-adjusted figure for 2001 was

$8,500.) Further, if the participant was engaged in more that one plan, they were limited to the same overall figure for such plans. Finally, any amount excluded under a 403(b) tax sheltered annuity had to be treated as an amount deferred for purposes of IRC section 457(b). Likewise, any amount excluded under a 401(k) plan, a salary reduction simplified employee pension (SEP) or contributed to a SIMPLE IRA had to be taken into account.

Effective for years beginning after December 31, 2001, the 2001 Tax Act deleted the requirement that IRC section 457(b) deferrals be coordinated with the contributions to the previous mentioned other types of plans, for purposes of determining a participant's contribution limit. In addition, the maximum deferral limit has been changed to a specific dollar amount (called the "applicable dollar amount") as follows:

For Tax Years Beginning In	Applicable Dollar Amount
2002	11,000
2003	12,000
2004	13,000
2005	14,000
2006 and thereafter	15,000

For this purpose the proposed regulations make it clear that the requirements of IRC section 457(b) apply to both elective contributions and other types of contributions such as mandatory contributions, nonelective employer contributions and matching employer contributions.

An eligible plan may allow a participant who attains age 50 by the end of the year to elect to have an additional deferral for the year. The additional amount permitted is $1,000 for 2002, $2,000 for 2003, $3,000 for 2004, $4,000 for 2005 and $5,000 for 2006. Further, a plan may permit a special larger catch up in the last three years before a participant attains normal retirement age. In that regard, pursuant to the 2001 Tax Act, for years after December 31, 2001, the most that can be deferred under this special

> An eligible plan may allow a participant who attains age 50 by the end of the year to elect to have an additional deferral for the year.

catch-up cannot exceed the lesser of (1) twice the applicable dollar amount, or (2) the sum of the otherwise applicable limit for the year plus the amount by which the limit applicable in preceding years of participation exceeded the deferrals for that year. For purposes of the application of these catch-up rules, the proposed regulations require that the plan designate a normal retirement age.

Distributions.

Payments may not be made to the participant or other beneficiary prior to when (1) the participant reaches age 70½, (2) the participant separates from service, or (3) the participant experiences an unforeseeable emergency. An unforeseeable emergency is defined as (1) a severe financial hardship resulting from a sudden and unexpected illness, or accident of the participant or a dependant, (2) a loss of the participant's property due to casualty, or (3) other similar or extraordinary and unforeseeable circumstances arising as a result of events which are beyond the control of the participant. The proposed regulations expand the definition of unforeseeable emergency to cover the loss of a principal residence, medical expenses, and the funeral expenses of a family member. In addition, the proposed regulations permit loans from governmental section 457 plans.

A section 457(b) plan is subject to the same minimum distribution requirements as apply to qualified plans under IRC section 409(a)(9). Prior to the 2001 Tax Act, 457 plans had to meet two additional requirements that did not apply to other plans. The 2001 Tax Act eliminated those additional requirements for distributions after December 31, 2001.

Timing of taxation.

Prior to the 2001 Tax Act, deferrals under section 457(b) plans and the income attributable to such deferrals were includible in gross income for the year that they were paid or otherwise "made available." Pursuant to the 2001 Tax Act, however, for distributions made after December 31, 2001, the timing of taxation for government plans and the plans of other tax-exempt organizations is to be distinguished as follows:

- **Government plans.** Deferrals and attributed income are includible in the gross income for the year *paid.*

- **Other tax-exempt organizations.** Deferrals and attributable income are included in the year *paid or otherwise made available.* This means that the participant or the participant's beneficiary can have no right to receive the income until the proscribed event. For example, the participant or beneficiary should not be given the right to accelerate the time for payment or have the right to assign the payment to another party.

Ownership of plan assets and income.

In the case of an eligible plan sponsored by a state or local government, all the assets and income must generally be held in a trust, custodial accounts, or annuity contracts for the exclusive benefit of participants or their beneficiaries.

> In the case of an eligible plan sponsored by a state or local government, all the assets and income must generally be held in a trust.

The trust, custodial or annuity requirement does not apply to the plans of nongovernmental, tax-exempt sponsors. The nongovernmental plans must provide, however, that all amounts deferred under the plans, all property and rights purchased with such amounts, and all the income thereon must belong solely to the plan sponsor but subject to the sponsor's general creditors. Further, while participants in such plans may not have a security interest in the plan's holdings, those assets may be placed in a "rabbi" trust for the participants' benefit. Finally, the participants may be given the right to select among various optional forms of investments that are offered under the plan as long as those investments are still subject to the claims of the plan sponsor's general creditors.

Life insurance owned by the plan.

The participants will not be charged with the value of life insurance protection under the plan as long as (1) the plan sponsor retains all of the incidents of ownership to the coverage, (2) the plan sponsor is the sole beneficiary, and (3) the plan sponsor is under no obligation to transfer the policy or its proceeds to the participants or their beneficiaries.

Any death benefits under the plan do not qualify for the exclusion from taxable income as life insurance proceeds under IRC section 101 and are taxable income to the recipient.

Plan to plan transfers and rollovers.

Under certain circumstances, amounts payable from one 457(b) plan can be "transferred" tax free to another 457(b) plan. (Note that the proposed regulations state that plan-to-plan transfers will not be permitted between government and tax-exempt 457(b) plans.)

> Under certain circumstances, amounts payable from one 457(b) plan can be "transferred" tax free to another 457(b) plan.

Prior to the 2001 Tax Act, however, distributions from a 457(b) plan did not qualify as "eligible rollover distributions," and therefore, could not be "rolled over" to another 457 plan, qualified plan, 403(b) annuity or IRA. Since this represented a serious limitation on the portability of *government* 457(b) plans the 2001 Tax Act extended the eligibility to receive tax-free rollovers to such plans under certain conditions after December 31, 2001. The price to be paid for this, however, is that with certain exceptions distributions from government 457 plans that are attributable to rollovers from a qualified plan, 403(b) annuity or IRA are subject to an early withdraw penalty of 10%.

IRC Section 457(b) Eligible Plan Diagram

The following is a diagram of what an eligible plan looks like:

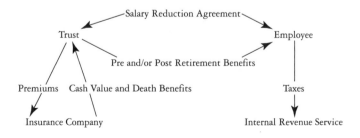

IRC Section 457(f) Ineligible Plans

Tax consequences.

Compensation deferred under an ineligible plan and the earnings thereon must be included in the participants' income, the later of when the services are performed, or when there is no longer a substantial risk of forfeiture. In this regard, the proposed regulations make it clear that once the deferred amounts and the earnings thereon are taxed any subsequent earnings are not taxable until they are paid or made available, as long as the participants remain only general creditors of the plan sponsor.

> It is important to note that plan sponsors may deliberately choose to establish a plan as an ineligible plan so as to avoid the contribution limits of eligible plans.

It is important to note that plan sponsors may deliberately choose to establish a plan as an ineligible plan so as to avoid the contribution limits of eligible plans. This is particularly true when the participants involved are highly compensated and the contribution limits of an eligible plan would not be adequate to meet their needs. An example of such a situation would be where highly paid physicians are providing services to a not for profit hospital corporation. In that case, the hospital could establish an ineligible plan and as long as the doctors' deferrals are subject to a substantial risk of forfeiture, they would not be subject to taxation until the deferrals become vested.

The same approach might be taken for highly paid state or local government employees as was done in the case covered by IRS Private Letter Ruling or "PLR" 9823014. In that situation, the top hat employees of a city council were covered by a deferred compensation arrangement that was not an eligible plan, and therefore, not subject to the then $33\frac{1}{3}\% - \$8,000$ limit because the plans assets were not placed in a trust. You should note that the employees' rights to the deferred amounts were subject to a substantial risk of forfeiture which delayed taxation until the employees' rights to the deferred amounts became vested.

IRC Section 457(f) Ineligible Plan Diagram

The following is a diagram of what an ineligible plan looks like:

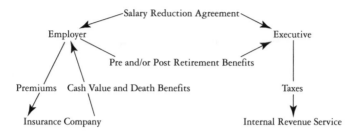

Sunset provision.

Note that the 2001 Tax Act contains a sunset provision that states that the above changes to the law that applied prior to 2002 will not apply after 2010.

Chapter 5

SPLIT DOLLAR LIFE INSURANCE

S plit dollar life insurance is a method of premium payment in which two parties agree to jointly pay the premiums on a life insurance policy. The purpose is to assist one party in acquiring coverage by having the other party contribute toward the cost of paying premiums. It may be used anytime that there is a need or desire to reduce the cost of coverage for one party and the other party is willing to contribute funds toward premium payments. As will be explained later, what distinguishes split dollar from other arrangements where one party assists another in paying premiums is that the contributing party is assured the return of all or part of its funds from either the policy's cash values or death proceeds. Examples of where it is used include providing family security, estate liquidity for paying death taxes and equalizing bequests to beneficiaries, informal funding of an employer's nonqualified deferred compensation plan, funding business buy and sell agreements, making charitable gifts, and leveraging private gifts.

Overview of the Three Phases of Split Dollar

The tax treatment of split dollar life insurance has gone through three major phases. Starting with the period from 1955 through 1964, it was viewed by the IRS as an interest free loan that had no tax consequences. Then in 1964, at Congressional urging, the Service decided that split dollar involved the transfer of a taxable economic benefit to employee participants in the form of current life insurance protection. During this second period from 1964 through 2001, employees were taxed on the value of life insurance protection, but debates raged over the proper method for valuing that protection and the issue of whether or not employees should be taxed on equity cash values that accrued for their benefit. Finally, in the third phase between 2001 and 2002, the IRS released two Notices and a Proposed Regulation that were intended to deal with, among other issues, the method for valuing current life insurance protection and the taxation of equity cash values.

Split Dollar Methods

With the beginning of the second phase that initiated the income taxation of split dollar, the IRS issued Rev. Rul. 64-328 in 1964. That Ruling held that split dollar provided a taxable economic benefit to employees in an amount equal to the one-year term cost of the decreasing life insurance protection to which they were entitled less the amount of any premiums they paid under their arrangements. Pursuant to Rev. Rul. 64-328, the one-year cost of insurance could be calculated using the "PS 58" table contained in Rev. Rul. 55-747, 1955-2 CB 228. Subsequently, in Rev. Rul. 66-110, the IRS gave taxpayers the option of using the insurer's term rates if they were generally available to all standard risks and lower than the PS 58 rates. In addition, Rev. Rul. 64-328 recognized two contractual forms of split dollar that were titled the "collateral assignment" and "endorsement" methods which may be described as follows.

> Rev. Rul. 64-328 recognized two contractual forms of split dollar that were titled the "collateral assignment" and "endorsement" methods.

Collateral assignment method.

In the conventional situation, the insured employee is the applicant and owner of the policy with the primary responsibility for the payment of premiums. The employer provides an amount each year equal to the annual increase in the policy's cash surrender value and the employee protects the employer's interest by collaterally assigning the policy to the employer. When the employee dies, the employer recovers the amount of the advances from the death proceeds under the collateral assignment and the employee's beneficiary receives the remainder. If the arrangement terminates before the employee's death, the employer's recovery is from the policy's cash surrender value pursuant to the collateral assignment.

Endorsement method.

Under the conventional approach, the employer is the applicant and owner of the policy with the primary responsibility for the payment of premiums. The employee reimburses the employer for the premiums in excess of the increase in the policy's cash surrender value. The employer is assured the return of its premium advances by designating itself beneficiary for that part of the death proceeds equal to the policy's cash surrender value. The employee names a personal beneficiary for the remainder. If the arrangement terminates during the employee's life, the employer can obtain the return of its premium advances through its control of cash values under the policy ownership endorsement.

> The employer is the applicant and owner of the policy with the primary responsibility for the payment of premiums.

Diagram of Methods

A diagram of the collateral assignment and endorsement methods is as follows:

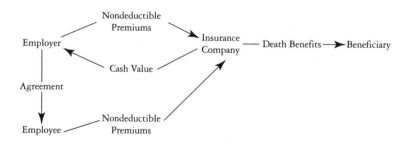

Taxation of Cash Values

Under the "classical" split dollar plan, whether the endorsement or collateral assignment approaches are used, the employer is given an interest in the policy equal to the greater of the policy's cash value or the aggregate premium contributions of the employer. This means that the employer obtains ownership of any cash values in excess of its premium contributions. Conversely, where the "equity" split dollar approach is applied the employer's interest in the cash values is limited to the extent of its total premium advances with any cash values in excess of that amount belonging to the employee. The consequence of giving the employee ownership of cash values in excess of the employer's premium advances raises the question of if, and when, such funds should be taxed to the employee. While this issue was not clearly addressed in Rev. Ruls. 64-328 or 66-110, in 1996 the IRS released Technical Advice Memorandum or TAM 9604001 which stated that any cash value that accumulated for the employee's benefit was also taxable to the employee as it accrued.

Notice 2001-10

TAM 9604001 caused considerable controversy and elicited much public comment that led to the release of Notice 2001-10 in January of 2001. Essentially, Notice 2001-10 was intended to provide interim guidance on equity plans and expressed the Services view that Rev. Ruls. 64-328 and 66-110 did not contemplate such arrangements. Consequently, pending public input and further guidance, the IRS offered taxpayers the choice of having their equity arrangements taxed under IRC section 7872 as an interest free loan or under IRC sections 61 and 83 as a transfer of economic benefits. A description of the tax consequences of those two approaches is as follows.

> The IRS offered taxpayers the choice of having their equity arrangements taxed under IRC section 7872 as an interest free loan or under IRC sections 61 and 83 as a transfer of economic benefits.

Loan treatment.

If the parties chose IRC section 7872 interest free loan treatment, the employee would not be taxed on the value of the life insurance protection or the cash surrender value that accrued for the employee's benefit. The employee's taxable income was to be calculated, however, using published government rates that determine the amount of forgone interest that would otherwise be paid by the employee to the employer on the loan.

Economic benefit treatment.

If the parties elected to have their agreement treated as an economic benefit the employee would be taxed annually on the value of their life insurance protection and also taxed on the amount of cash value owned by the employee upon termination of the arrangement.

IRS Notice 2002-8

On January 3, 2002, the IRS released Notice 2002-8, which revoked Notice 2001-10 and announced that the Service intended to publish proposed regulations that would provide comprehensive guidance on the Federal tax treatment of split dollar life insurance arrangements. Notice 2002-8 states that those regulations will apply to split dollar arrangements entered into after the regulations are published in final form. Further, reminiscent of prior Notice 2001-10, Notice 2002-8 provides that taxpayers will be required to treat their arrangements as either interest free loans under IRC sections 7872 or as transfers of economic benefits that are taxable to the employee under IRC sections 61 and 83. Note that if an employee is not required to repay the employer's premium payments the arrangement will not be treated as a split dollar arrangement under either approach and the employee will be taxed on the premium payments when made by the employer.

A major difference between Notices 2001-10 and 2002-8 is that pursuant to 2002-8, the tax treatment under the proposed regulations was expected to hinge on which party was "formally designated" as the owner of the life insurance policy. Consequently, if the collateral assignment method were used the arrangement would be treated as a interest free loan subject to IRC section 7872 since the employee would be designated as the owner. The employer might also have tax considerations under the original issue discount rules of IRC sections 1271-1275. Conversely, if the employer was designated as the owner, under the endorsement method, the employee would be taxed on (1) the value of their current life insurance protection under IRC section 61 and (2) any equity cash values going to the employee, at termination of the arrangement, under IRC sections 83.

Safe harbor rules.

Notice 2002-8 states that the regulations will only apply to arrangements entered into after the regulations are published in final form. This means that the new rules do not apply to split dollar arrangements that existed when the Notice was released or those that are entered into before the regulations are published in final form. In regard to such arrangements, Notice 2002-8 provides considerable grandfather protection through a series of safe harbor rules described below. Note that the Notice uses the terms "service recipient" and "sponsor" to describe the party providing premium advances or loans. However, since that is usually the role of an employer, for the sake of simplicity, the term "employer" will be used to describe that party. Further, the Notice uses the terms "service provider" and "benefited party" to describe the role usually held by an employee. Consequently, the term "employee" will be used to describe that party:

> Notice 2002-8 provides considerable grandfather protection through a series of safe harbor rules.

- **Equity cash values not taxed as they accrue.** The sole fact that a policy develops cash values in excess of what is payable to the employer, for its premium advances, will not cause those excess or "equity" amounts to be taxed to the employee. This specifically rejects the position taken in TAM 9604001, whereby the employee would have been taxed currently on equity cash values as they accrued.

- **No taxation of cash values until rollout.** As long as the value of current life insurance protection is reported to the employee as taxable income, the split dollar arrangement will not be treated as having been terminated. The rule applies regardless of the interest that the employer has remaining in the policy. This means that as long as the employee continues to recognize the value of life insurance protection as taxable income, the IRS will not try to treat the arrangement as terminated and tax the equity cash value to the employee under IRC section 83 even though the employer's interest has been paid off. While this seems to say that the employer does not have to retain any interest in the policy to keep the employee from being taxed on the employee's share of cash value, it may be wise for the employer to have at least a small amount of interest in the policy.

- **All premium advances treated as loans.** The parties may choose to have their split dollar arrangement treated as an interest free loan from its inception, if they report all the employer's prior premium advances (less repayments) as loans in the first tax year that such loan treatment is adopted. This means that for the employee the arrangement will be governed by IRC sections 7872 and for the employer sections 1271–1275 may apply with the understanding that the IRS will not challenge reasonable efforts to comply with those rules.

> The parties may choose to have their split dollar arrangement treated as an interest free loan from its inception.

- **Termination of arrangement before January 1, 2004.** For split dollar arrangements entered into before January 28, 2002 (where the employer has made premium or other payments and has received or is entitled to receive full repayment) the IRS will not apply IRC section 83 to tax the employee on equity cash values at termination ("rollout") of the arrangement if the arrangement is terminated before January 1, 2004. The ability under this safe harbor to terminate a split dollar arrangement before January 1, 2004, without having IRC section 83 apply, means that split dollar arrangements may by unwound or "rolled out" before that date without having to recognize the employee's share of cash value as income.

- **Loan treatment after January 1, 2004.** The IRS will not take the position that there has been a transfer of property under IRC section 83 upon termination of an arrangement if, for all periods beginning on or after January 1, 2004, all the employer's payments from the inception of the arrangement (less repayments) are treated as loans. Further, any such payment by the employer before the first taxable year in which such payments are treated as loans for federal tax purposes must be treated as loans entered into at the beginning of that first year in which such payments are treated as loans. This means that IRC section 7872 will apply to the employee and sections 1271–1275 may apply to the employer.

- **No inference from Notice 2002-8 for prefinal regulation agreements.** Except for the new rules governing the valuation of current life insurance protection that follow, Part IV of Notice 2002-8 states that "no inference should be drawn from this notice regarding the appropriate Federal income, employment and gift tax treatment of split dollar life insurance arrangements entered into before the date of publication of final regulations. This seems to allow taxpayers who do not elect the protection of one of the safe harbors to argue that their arrangements are governed by Rev. Rul. 64-328, which makes no mention of the taxation of equity cash values under IRC section 83. By the same token, the IRS seems to be allowed to argue that section 83 does apply to such arrangements. In any case, Notice 2002-8 states that taxpayers may rely on it (including a reasonable interpretation of the following rules on computing the value of current life insurance protection) or Notice 2001-10 for reporting the tax treatment of split dollar arrangements entered into before the final regulations are published.

Valuing Current Life Insurance Protection

With regard to measuring the value of current life insurance protection, IRS Notice 2001-10 denied the use of PS 58 rates after 2001, created a new table ("Table 2001"—based on IRC section 79 rates for group term life insurance) for measuring the value of current insurance protection and limited the use of an insurer's alternative term rates pending further guidance.

As previously stated, IRS Notice 2002-8 revoked Notice 2001-10 and provides that pending the publication of further guidance, the following interim guidance applies for determining the value of current life insurance protection that an employee enjoys under a split dollar arrangement:

- **Revocation/grand fathering of PS 58 rates.** The use of PS 58 rates after 2001 is generally prohibited. PS 58 rates may continue to be used, however, for split dollar arrangements in effect before January 28, 2002, if a contractual agreement between the employee and the employer provides for the use of PS 58 rates.

- **Table 2001 rates.** For arrangements entered into before the final regulations are published, taxpayers may use the Table 2001 rates that were first published in Notice 2001-10. In addition, taxpayers should make appropriate adjustments to the Table 2001 rates if the life insurance protection covers more than one life. With regard to second-to-die policies, there is no formal authority from the IRS on how to measure the value of such insurance under split dollar arrangements. The only guidance prior to Notice 2001-10 came from what is referred to as the "Greenberg to Greenberg" letter of August 10, 1983, and subsequent IRS information letters that used the so-called "PS 38" rate while both insureds are alive. After the first death the Table 2001 rate would presumable apply. The problem is that the PS 38 Table is directly related to the PS 58 table that no longer applies. This means that taxpayers are left on their own in trying to extrapolate second-to-die rates from Table 2001.

> Taxpayers should make appropriate adjustments to the Table 2001 rates if the life insurance protection covers more than one life.

- **Alternative term rates.** For arrangements entered into before the publication of final regulations, taxpayers may continue to use the insurer's lower published premium rates (alternative term rates) that are available to all standard risks for initial issue one-year term insurance. However, as to arrangements entered into after January 28, 2002, and before the publication of final regulations, for periods after December 31, 2003, the IRS will not respect such rates unless:

The insurer generally makes the availability of such rates known to persons who apply for term insurance from the insurer, and

The insurer regularly sells term insurance at such rates to individuals who apply for term insurance through the insurer's normal distribution channels.

While these standards do not apply to arrangements entered into before January 28, 2002, it does not mean that the IRS will not challenge an insurer's alternative term rates on the basis that they are not generally available to all standard risks as required by Rev. Rul. 66-110.

Split Dollar Proposed Regulations (REG. 164754-01, 26 CFR Parts 1 and 31)

On July 3, 2002, the IRS released the Proposed Regulations described in Notice 2002-8. They are stated to apply to employer/employee, corporation/shareholder, and donor/donee split dollar arrangements. Consequently, in their final form, they will govern split dollar for purposes of Federal income, employment, and gift tax purposes. Further, they generally adopt the tax treatment described in Notice 2002-8 but include some modifications and additions. Most significantly, they are prospective in application and will not take effect until after the publication of final regulations. In the interim, taxpayers can rely upon Notice 2002-8 including the grandfathering protection described above. The principal provisions of the Proposed Regulations are as follows.

Definition of "split dollar life insurance."

The Proposed Regulations define "split dollar" as any arrangement that is not group term life insurance between an owner of a life insurance contract and a nonowner of the contract under which either party to the arrangement pays all or part of the premiums and, one of the parties paying the premiums is entitled to recover (either conditionally or unconditionally) all or any portion of those premiums and such recovery is to be made from, or is secured by, the proceeds of the contract. In regard to the interpretation of this definition, the preamble to the Proposed Regulations states that it is to be applied broadly, and that the amount to be recovered by the party paying the premiums need not be determined by reference to the amount of the premiums.

> There is a special rule for those cases entered into in connection with the performance of services.

66

Further, there is a special rule for those cases entered into in connection with the performance of services. For that purpose, split dollar is any arrangement between a owner and a nonowner under which the employer or service recipient pays, directly or indirectly all or a portion of the premiums and the beneficiary of all or any portion of the death benefit is designated by the employee or service provider or is any person whom the employee or service provider would reasonable be expected name as a beneficiary. This also applies between a corporation and a shareholder.

Definition of policy "owner" and "nonowner."

In general, the "owner" of a life insurance policy is defined by the Proposed Regulation as the person named as the policy owner. On the other hand, the "nonowner" is any person other than the owner who has a direct or indirect interest in the policy. In addition, if two or more persons are designated as owners and each person has an undivided interest in every right and benefit they are treated as owners of separate contracts and neither contract will be treated as a split dollar arrangement. Finally, if two or more persons are designated as policy owners and each person does not have all the incidents of ownership as to an undivided interest in the contract, the person who is named first is treated as the owner.

There are two exceptions to the above rules that apply to nonequity arrangements. First, the employer or service recipient is treated as the owner at all times if the only economic benefit to the employee or service provider is current life insurance protection. Second, in donor/donee situations the donor is treated as the owner if the only economic benefit to the donee is current life insurance protection.

Overview of the tax treatment of split dollar under the proposed regulations.

Generally, the Proposed Regulations continue the tax regime laid out in Notices 2001-10 and 2002-8 by giving taxpayers the choice of structuring their arrangements under the endorsement method as a transfer of economic benefits from the owner to the nonowner or as a collateral assignment method interest free loan from the nonowner to the owner. The specific tax consequences flowing from each arrangement then depends on the relationship of the parties, that is, employer/employee, corporation/shareholder, or donor/donee, as explained next.

Endorsement method economic benefit arrangements.

The endorsement method economic benefit arrangements are structured with the employer, corporation, or donor formally designated as the owner of the contract while the employee, shareholder, or donee is designated as the nonowner. For tax purposes, the Proposed Regulations separate these endorsement arrangements into equity and nonequity types as follows:

- **Nonequity endorsement method split dollar.** The value of current life insurance protection paid for by the owner (employer, corporation, or donor) less the amount of the nonowner's (employee, shareholder, or donee) premium contribution is treated as compensation, a dividend, or a gift. For purposes of calculating the amount of the current life insurance protection the Proposed Regulations require the use of a "life insurance premium factor designated or permitted in guidance published in the Internal Revenue Bulletin." (Currently that is Table 2001.) Interestingly, the Proposed Regulation deals with policies that have the potential for changing the amount of death benefits during the year. That is accomplished by defining the amount of current life insurance protection to the nonowner as the excess of the "average" death benefit over the total amount payable to the owner. Further, the total amount payable to the owner is increased by the amount of any outstanding policy loan. Finally, the Proposed Regulations make no mention of using the insurer's lower term rates for calculating the amount of current life insurance protection. Presumably, the grandfathering rules under Notice 2002-8 explained above would still apply.

> The amount of the "annual increase" in the value of the nonowner's interest in the policy's equity must be taken into account.

- **Equity endorsement method split dollar.** Under this approach the current value of life insurance protection is compensation to the employee, a dividend to the shareholder, and a gift to the donee. In addition, the amount of the "annual increase" in the value of the nonowner's interest in the policy's equity must be taken into account. This means that for the employee it is compensation, for the shareholder it is a dividend, and for the donee it is a gift. The way to measure the nonowner's annual share of the increase in equity is not described but the IRS asks for comments on this issue. In addition, it offers the possibility of subtracting from current premium payments made by the contract owner the net present value of the amount to be repaid to the owner in the future. Significantly, this represents a change from what was set forth in Notices 2001-10 and 2002-8 since the nonowners interest in the equity would have to be recognized annually and not at rollout.

Tax treatment of loans, withdrawals, dividends, and so on under the endorsement method.

The nonowner (employee, shareholder, or donee) is also accountable on any amount received under the policy as a loan, withdraw, or dividend. The situation is treated as thought the amount in question was first paid to the owner (employer, corporation, or donor) and then paid by the owner to the nonowner (employee, shareholder, or donee). This results in taxation to the owner in accordance with the rules of IRC section 72 and then compensation, a dividend, or a gift to the nonowner. In that regard, the amount of compensation, dividend, or gift to the nonowner is reduced by the amount previously taken into taxable income by the nonowner as economic benefit or paid by the nonowner for the economic benefit. Note that this reduction does not include the value of current life insurance protection taken into account by the nonowner or paid for by the nonowner.

> The nonowner is also accountable on any amount received under the policy as a loan, withdraw, or dividend.

Tax basis in the policy under the endorsement method.

Under the proposed Regulation the nonowner does not receive a tax basis for premiums paid or the value of current life insurance protection taken into income. In the past, the IRS has given vague signals on the subject of using employee premium contributions to both offset imputed income and add to the employee's basis in the contract. This is because, while not clear on the subject, PLR 7916029 has generally been interpreted to mean that the contribution added to basis cannot also be used to offset imputed income from life insurance protection. Further, in PLR 8310027, the IRS stated that the employee's contributions could be added to basis but made no mention of their also being used to offset imputed income from the insurance protection.

Transfer of the life insurance contract under the endorsement method.

Where a policy or an undivided interest in a policy is transferred from the owner to the nonowner, the nonowner is taxable under IRC section 83 on the fair market value (generally the cash surrender value) of the contract, less the sum of any consideration paid for the contract and income previously recognized from the equity on the contract. In the employer/employee context, the employer gets an income tax deduction for the compensation income recognized by the employee. Further, the transferee nonowner receives a tax basis in the contract equal to the greater of the fair market value of the contract or the sum of the amount the transferee pays to obtain the contract plus the amount of unrecovered economic benefits previously taken into account or paid for by the transferee. Note that this tax basis does not include any income previously taken into account for current life insurance protection or any amount paid for such protection.

Contributory endorsement method arrangements.

The Proposed Regulations contain a new rule that any amount paid for current life insurance protection by the nonowner is income to the owner. This even applies to donor/donee gift situations.

Tax treatment of endorsement method death benefits.

Under the Proposed Regulations the death benefit portion that is attributable to the amount of income recognized by the nonowner or paid for by the nonowner is income tax free to the beneficiary under IRC section 101. However, the amount paid at death that represents the nonowners interest in the cash value in excess of the nonowners basis for that amount seems to be taxable income to the beneficiary.

Collateral assignment interest free loan arrangements.

Pursuant to the Proposed Regulations if the employee, shareholder, or donee is named as the policy owner and is required to repay the nonowner (employer, corporation, or donor) out of the policy proceeds or otherwise, the nonowner's premium contributions will be treated as a series of loans and subject to IRC section 7872 and where applicable the original issue discount rules of IRC sections 1271–1275. In that regard, it should be noted that the IRS recognizes that in the early years of the arrangement the surrender value of the policy may be less than the loan resulting in under collateralization but so long as a reasonable person would expect the repayment to be made in full, the premium payments are a split dollar loan under Reg. 1.7872-15. For this purpose, any portion of the premium contributions by the nonowner, that are not repayable (or not reasonably expected to be repaid) are not treated like a split dollar loan and are taxable to the owner under IRC section 61. Further, the "de minimus" rule of IRC section 7872 that exempts loans not exceeding $10,000 does not apply to split dollar loans.

> The "de minimus" rule of IRC section 7872 that exempts loans not exceeding $10,000 does not apply to split dollar loans.

Indirect collateral assignment loans.

In those cases involving indirect loans to a third party, the Proposed Regulations treat the situation as a series of successive or back-to-back loans the tax treatment of which depends on the relationships of the parties. For example, where an employer (nonowner) advances premiums to an employee's irrevocable life insurance trust (owner), the forgone interest is computed as if the employer made loans to the employee (taxable as compensation) and the employee then loaned the same amounts to the trust (reportable as gifts).

Nonrecourse collateral assignment method loans.

> **Written representation must be attached to the parties' tax returns for the first year a loan is made.**

The proposed regulations state that if the loan is nonrecourse as to the borrower (as split dollar loans typically are), it will be treated as a "contingent payment." Since this has negative implications when testing for "adequate interest," as explained next, the parties may choose to avoid such a characterization by providing for stated interest and representing in writing that a reasonable person would expect that all payments under the loan will be made. The written representation must be attached to the parties' tax returns for the first year a loan is made.

Collateral assignment demand loans versus term loans.

For purposes of the application of the rules under IRC section 7872, split dollar loans are generally classified as "demand loans" or "term loans" by the Proposed Regulations. Their respective tax treatments are as follows.

Demand loans.

This type of split dollar loan is defined as any split dollar loan that is payable in full at any time on the demand of the lender. For purposes of taxation, each year the loan is tested for adequate stated interest under IRC section 7872. It will be deemed to have adequate stated interest if the interest rate is no lower than the "annual blended rate" (an average of the January and July short term rates that is published each June) for the year based on annual compounding. If the loan does not have adequate stated interest, the forgone interest will be treated as though it was transferred from the lender to the borrower on the last day of the calendar year and characterized for tax purposes according to the relationships of the parties. This means that it will be compensation to an employee, a dividend to a shareholder, and a gift to a donee. That amount is then treated as being retransferred from the borrower to the lender as nondeductible interest on the last day of the calendar year.

Term loans.

This type of loan is defined as any split dollar loan that is not a demand loan and such loans are tested on the day the loan is made to determine if it has adequate stated interest. For this purpose, interest is adequate if the face amount of the loan is equal to or greater than the imputed loan amount. The "imputed loan amount" is defined as the present value of all payments due under the loan as of the date the loan is made, using a discount rate equal to the applicable federal rate or "AFR," on that date. The loan's term is the period from the date it is made to its stated maturity date. The difference between the loans face amount and the imputed loan amount is compensation to an employee and a dividend to a shareholder. The amount recognized as income by the borrower is Original Issue Discount to the lender and taken into income ratably over the term of the loan (IRC sections 1271–1275).

There is special treatment for the forgone interest on term loans payable at death, gift term loans (only for income tax purposes) and term loans conditioned on the performance of substantial future services. The forgone interest on such term loans is to be determined annually in a manner that is similar to demand loans but using an AFR that matches the loan's term and is determined when the loan is made.

Note that for a loan payable on death, the loan's term is determined with reference to the individual's life expectancy, using the appropriate table under the regulations to IRC section 72. Further, for gift loans, the term is from when it is made until its stated maturity date. In addition, while the income tax consequences of the gift loan are determined like a demand loan (annually), the gift tax results are decided in accordance with term loan treatment. This means that generally, the difference between the face amount and the imputed loan amount is a gift to the donee in the year the loan is made. Finally, with respect to loans conditioned on the performance of substantial future services, the term is based on its stated maturity date and if none is stated, the term is deemed to be 7 years.

Modifications to a split dollar agreement.

Even though the Proposed Regulations will not be effective until published in final form, any arrangement entered into before that date that is materially modified after the regulations are effective will be treated as a new arrangement that is entered into on the date of the modification. This means that split dollar arrangements that would not otherwise be subject to the final regulations can become subject to them if they are materially changed after the regulations effective date.

Premium payment variations.

Additional flexibility in the design of a split dollar plan can be obtained through variations from the conventional premium arrangement in which the employer advances the annual increase in the policy's cash value. Examples include:

> Flexibility in the design of a split dollar plan can be obtained through variations from the conventional premium arrangement in which the employer advances the annual increase in the policy's cash value.

- **Employer pay all.** The employer pays the entire premium. This is attractive to the employee because it requires less of a financial outlay by the employee. To the employer there is some risk, however, of a loss of its funds if the arrangement terminates before the policy's cash value equals the employer's premium advances. Note that the case of *Genshaft v. Commissioner,* 64 TC 282 (1975) held that such arrangements are split dollar plans.

- **Economic benefit.** The employee pays a portion of the premium equal to the economic benefit that would otherwise be taxed to the employee and the employer pays the rest. Initially, this approach may require a lesser outlay for the employee than under the conventional arrangement but as the employee grows older, the taxable economic benefit to the employee will increase to a point where it is no longer economical to the employee and the arrangement will typically be terminated or "rolled out," as explained later.

- **Level premium.** The employee pays a level amount of premium each year and the employer pays the balance. Evening out the employee's contributions makes the plan more affordable to the employee but puts the employer's security interest at risk in the early years when its premium advances exceed the policy's cash value.

- **Reverse split dollar.** In this split dollar arrangement, the traditional roles of the employer and employee are reversed in that the employee's beneficiary is entitled to a portion of the death benefit equal to the policy's cash value and the employer is entitled to the balance. In addition, the employee owns all of the cash value and the employer pays a portion of the premium reflecting the cost of its share of the death proceeds. Consequently, it is an appropriate choice where the provision of cash values to the employee and key protection to the employer are primary goals of the parties in establishing a split dollar program. When the arrangement is terminated, the employer ceases to make further premium contributions and gives up its right to a portion of the death benefit.

IRS Notice 2001-10 stated that the Service is concerned that in some cases the employer's share of the premium has been overstated resulting in economic benefits to the employee in excess of what is properly allocated to the employee's share of the premium. Specifically, the IRS stated that this occurs when the employer's share of premiums is determined using PS 58 rates for which there is no published guidance authorizing the use of such rates. Moreover, footnote 1 to the preamble to the Proposed Regulations specifically states that taxpayers may not use PS 58 rates for reverse split dollar arrangements (or private noncompensatory split dollar arrangements). Finally, on August 16, 2002, the Service released Notice 2002-59, which seems to prohibit the use of PS 58 rates, Table 2001 rates or an insurer's alternative term rates for measuring the value of life insurance protection in reverse split dollar arrangements. Further, the Notice takes the position that the IRS has always opposed the use of government tables or insurers' alternative term rates as a means of measuring, for income and gift tax purposes, the amount of cash values that accrue for the benefit of an employee under reverse split dollar arrangements. Moreover, Notice 2002-59 does not contain a prospective effective date, transition rules, or a method for measuring the cash value accruing for the benefit of an employee under a reverse split dollar arrangement. This seems to leave to litigation, or possibly the final regulations, the determination of how reverse split dollar arrangements are to be treated for income and gift tax purposes. The bottom line seems to be that until resolved by litigation, or final regulations, any prospective cases involving premium payment approaches that are specifically designed to increase the employer's share of the premiums should be approached with caution. Examples of such arrangements are having the employer or donor prepay its premiums or pay averaged premiums instead of normally increasing premiums.

- **Flexible premium products.** Any of the previous premium payment variations can be applied to interest sensitive and variable premium as well as traditional type insurance products. Those policies would, however, pose special considerations with regard to the responsibility for making incremental allocations for variable contracts and choosing the funding levels for flexible premium and universal life policies.

Application of Dividends.

> The application of dividends on a participating policy offers great flexibility in tailoring a plan to the needs of the parties.

The application of dividends on a participating policy offers great flexibility in tailoring a plan to the needs of the parties. In this regard, split dollar plans are frequently established using dividends to purchase paid up additions with any balance used to purchase one of the other options. Without the supplementary paid up additions, the beneficiary of the employee, shareholder, or donee would receive a decreasing share of the death benefit as the share going to the employer, corporation, or donor increased in accordance with its cumulative premium advances. A similar result can be achieved using one-year-term insurance where it is available from the insurer.

Dividend treatment.

The Proposed Regulations state that once they become effective in final form, Rev. Rul. 66-110 will become obsolete. (See above for the tax treatment of dividends under the Proposed Regulations.) Prior to that time, however, Rev. Rul. 66-110 provides that the economic benefits that result to an employee through the application of various dividend options are taxed as follows:

- **Cash dividend to employee.** The amount of the dividend is included in the employee's income.

- **One-year term provided to employee.** The employee recognizes the amount of the dividend as income.

- **Paid-up insurance.** Where the employee owns the cash value of the PUA, as well as the right to designate the beneficiary of that coverage, the employee is taxed on the full amount of the dividend so applied. Where, however, the employer owns the cash value of the PUA, the employee is only taxed on the value of the insurance protection provided to the employee's beneficiary by the PUA using Table 2001 or the insurer's alternative term rates.

- **Reduce premiums.** Rev. Rul. 66-110 did not discuss this option, but it is generally assumed that where it reduces the employee's share of the premium, it is taxed to the employee. Where it reduces the employer's share of the premium, however, it is not taxed to either party.

Rollout.

Split dollar arrangements are usually terminated on the following events:

- The death of the insured employee.

- Termination of the employee's employment.

- Surrender of the policy.

- The imputed income from the arrangement makes it uneconomical as a form of premium payment. This would occur when the imputed income from the insurance protection reaches the cross over point and starts to exceed the premium.

> Terminating the arrangement for reasons other than the employee's death is referred to as "rollout" and is normally planned for when the split dollar arrangement is established.

Terminating the arrangement for reasons other than the employee's death is referred to as "rollout" and is normally planned for when the split dollar

77

arrangement is established. The most likely occasions for rollout are the employee's retirement or the reaching the crossover point where imputed income starts to exceed the policy premium. Rollout involves the employee paying off the employer's interest in the policy through the use of policy cash values or some other source of funds that is available to the employee. Upon the employer being repaid by the employee, the employer's interest in the policy is terminated. It should be noted that, as provided in the safe harbor provisions previously discussed, IRS Notice 2002-8 seems to allow all split dollar arrangements to be unwound before January 1, 2004, without the employee having to recognize income under IRC section 83 on the employee's share of cash values.

Illustration of concept.

The table on page 75 of an actual policy may not to be used with the public but shows the operation and rollout of a split dollar agreement. The policy is a universal life type and the assumptions are that it reflects nonguaranteed results based on an interest rate of 6.65% and current charges. It is a $1,000,000 Type A fixed death benefit with an initial annual premium outlay of $13,174. Further, assume that it covers a 46-year-old male nonsmoker in the 40% tax bracket who is employed by a corporation in the 34% bracket. Finally, assume that pursuant to the Proposed Regulations the employee is taxed annually in regard to "equity" cash values that are owned by the employee.

Transfer for value.

Care must be taken upon the creation or termination of a split dollar arrangement that a "transfer for value" does not occur since this would cause all or part of the death proceeds to loose their income tax free status under IRC section 101(a)(1). In this regard, IRC section 101(a)(2) provides that if a transfer of any interest in a life insurance policy is made for a valuable consideration, the death proceeds will be subject to taxation to the extent they exceed the sum of the consideration and any subsequent premiums paid by the transferee.

There are two types of exceptions to the transfer for value rule. The first includes transfers by gift to anyone and the second is for transfers to

		Employer			Employee		
Year	Age	Split Annual Outlay* ($)	Cash Value ($)	Death Benefit ($)	Split Annual Outlay** ($)	Cash Value ($)	Death Benefit ($)
1	46	13,174	0	13,174	253	0	986,826
2	47	13,174	6,590	26,348	265	0	973,652
3	48	13,174	18,276	39,522	277	0	960,478
4	49	13,174	30,571	52,696	292	0	947,304
5	50	13,174	43,537	65,870	306	0	934,130
6	51	13,174	57,208	79,044	324	0	920,956
7	52	13,174	71,608	92,218	341	0	907,782
8	53	13,174	86,749	105,392	361	0	894,608
9	54	13,174	102,651	118,566	384	0	881,434
10	55	13,174	119,332	131,740	406	0	868,260
11	56	13,174	137,757	144,914	431	0	855,086
12	57	13,174	157,108	158,088	458	0	841,912
13	58	13,174	171,262	171,262	2,956	6,180	828,738
14	59	13,174	184,436	184,436	3,855	14,537	815,564
15	60	13,174	197,610	197,610	4,397	24,175	802,390
16	61	13,174	210,784	210,784	4,980	35,181	789,216
17	62	13,174	223,958	223,958	5,630	47,710	776,042
18	63	13,174	237,132	237,132	6,323	61,863	762,868
19	64	13,174	250,306	250,306	7,010	77,618	749,694
20	65	−250,306	0	0	13,174	91,458	749,669
Total		0			52,423		

*The employer's "Split Annual Outlay" is the premium the employer pays for the first 19 years before rollout. Then in year 20 the employer receives its $250,306 share of cash value upon rollout and pays no further premiums.

**The employee's "Split Annual Outlay" is the tax at a 40% rate that the employee pays on the imputed income from the life insurance protection and the employee's share of the annual increase in cash value before rollout in years 1–19. Then the employee pays the premium of $13,174 in year 20, as after rollout the employee carries the policy on his own paying the $13,174 annual premium.

Note: The Proposed Regulations do not contain specific instructions on how to compute the annual tax on the employee's interest in the policy's equity. The IRS merely offers the "possibility" of subtracting from current premium payments made by the contract owner the net present value of the amount to be repaid to the owner in the future. In addition, on May 8, 2003 the IRS released supplementary proposed regulations that would tax the employee each year on the employee's share of the case value without an offset for the amount of cash value recognized as income in prior years.

certain parties. Regarding the exception for certain parties the transfers covered are those to the insured, to a partner of the insured, to a partnership in which the insured is a partner, or to a corporation in which the insured is a shareholder or officer.

In any case, when setting up or dissolving a split dollar arrangement, extreme care must be taken that any shifts of interests in the policy fit into one of the above exceptions. For example, if an existing policy is owned by a corporation and transferred to the insured to start an IRC section 7872 type of interest free loan arrangement there will be no problem because transfers to the insured are exempt from the rule. Similarly, a transfer to the corporation by the insured to begin a split dollar endorsement arrangement would be exempt if the insured were an officer or shareholder of the corporation. Likewise, when the policy is formally transferred to the insured at termination or rollout of the endorsement arrangement, there is no problem since transfers to the insured are exempt. On the other hand, a transfer to a third party will not be exempt unless it meets one of the exceptions such as where the transferee is a partner of the insured under a separate partnership business.

> When setting up or dissolving a split dollar arrangement, extreme care must be taken.

Nondeductible premiums and income tax free death proceeds.

Rev. Rul. 64-328 states that an employer is not entitled to any deduction for its share of the annual premiums. In addition, the Ruling states that the death proceeds received by the employer and the employee's beneficiary are exempt from income taxation. Note that the Proposed Regulations make Rev. Rul. 64-328 obsolete as of the effective date of final regulations. In any case, the Proposed Regulations state that IRC section 264(a)(1) provides that no deduction is allowed for premiums on any life insurance policy if the taxpayer is directly or indirectly a beneficiary under the policy. As to the tax treatment of death proceeds under the Proposed Regulations, see previously under "Tax treatment of endorsement method death benefits."

Accumulated earnings tax and alternative minimum tax.

Regarding the impact of split dollar arrangements on a corporation's exposure to the accumulated earnings tax (IRC Sections 531–537); such plans may contribute to creating a liability when the corporation's share of cash values exceed its premium contributions as may occur under the previously mentioned "classical" approach. Even in those situations, however, the problem may be avoided if the accumulations are needed to fund various employee benefits or key person insurance protection. This is because additions to accumulated earnings for the "reasonable needs" of the business are exempt from the tax. Similarly, when the employer's share of cash value is limited to its premium contributions through an "equity" arrangement, the exposure appears to be eliminated. Likewise, liability for the corporate alternative minimum tax (IRC sections 55–59) would seem to turn on the corporation's right to cash values or death proceeds in excess of its contributions which may be avoided under the equity approach. Note that the Taxpayers Relief Act of 1997 exempts small corporations that meet a gross receipts test from the tax.

Shareholder split dollar.

Besides establishing split dollar plans for employees, a corporation may choose to enter into such arrangements with nonemployee stockholders. In such cases, the IRS provided through Rev. Rul. 79-50, 1978-1 CB 138, that the arrangement would be treated like an employer-employee split dollar arrangement, except that the value of the insurance protection was deemed a corporate distribution (dividend) to the shareholders instead of compensation. It should be noted that the Proposed Regulations make Rev. Rul. 79-50 obsolete as of the effective date of final regulations. The tax treatment of shareholders under the Proposed Regulations is explained previously with regard to endorsement method and collateral assignment method split dollar arrangements.

Subchapter S corporations.

Subchapter S status creates a unique difference in the distinction between contributory and noncontributory split dollar plans. In the case of a noncontributory plan the employee shareholder is subjected to a form of double taxation. This is because the employee must recognize taxable income on both the passed through nondeductible premium contribution and the imputed income for the value of the life insurance coverage. Contributory plans (endorsement plans under the Proposed Regulations) avoid this double trap since the employee shareholder may offset the imputed income with premium contributions. The amount of income passed through to the insured from the corporation's nondeductible premium contribution depends on the percentage of the insured's ownership interest in the corporation. This means that if the insured owns less than 100% of the corporation, some of the cost of the insured's coverage will be born by other shareholders in proportion to their ownership interest. Consequently, split dollar in the context of Subchapter S corporations from a tax perspective probably only makes sense for minority shareholders or nonshareholder employees. On the other hand, depending on what the parties are trying to accomplish, it might be advisable for substantial or sole shareholders for nontax reasons when established as part of a larger estate planning picture.

> Subchapter S status creates a unique difference in the distinction between contributory and noncontributory split dollar plans.

Caution must be taken that the creation of a split dollar arrangement for a Sub S shareholder does not create a second class of stock. This is because such corporations are only permitted one class of stock and if the economic benefits stemming from the split dollar plan are deemed to create another class of stock for the covered shareholder(s) the Sub S election is automatically revoked. In this regard the IRS has held in a number of Private Letter Rulings that there is no second class of stock if the corporation is reimbursed for the value of the insurance protection received by the covered shareholder. See PLRs 9331009, 9309046, 9413023, 9651017, and 9735006. The bottom line from these rulings seems to be that in order to be safe from the second class of stock issue, the corporation must be reimbursed for the value of the economic benefit received by the covered shareholder(s).

Estate Tax Consequences

Inclusion of death proceeds in the insured's gross estate.

IRC section 2042 provides that if the insured has any incidents of ownership in the policy at the time of death, either alone or in conjunction with any other person, the proceeds are includible in the insured's estate for federal estate tax purposes. This was confirmed by the Tax court in the case of *Eleanor M. Schwager,* 64 TC 781 (1975) in which the court held that the incidents of ownership rules do apply to split dollar life insurance. The facts of the case were that the employer owned a policy of life insurance on the employee's life. The employer was the beneficiary of the proceeds equal to the cash value and the employee's widow was the beneficiary for the balance. The employer could not change the beneficiary of the proceeds in excess of the cash value without the employee's consent. The Tax court held that the employee's right to consent was an incident of ownership and ruled that the death proceeds were included in his estate without stating clearly whether all the proceeds should be included or just that portion payable to his widow beneficiary. Note that if all the proceeds are included in the estate, there may be an offsetting deduction under IRC section 2053 for the amount of proceeds paid to the employer.

Triangular split dollar.

A means of avoiding the inclusion of split dollar death proceeds in the insured's estate is to establish a "triangular "split dollar plan in which a third party enters into the split dollar arrangement with the employer. Under this approach, the insured possesses no incidents of ownership that could cause the proceeds to be included in his or her estate. (See Rev. Rul. 78-420, 1978-2 CB 67.) You should note, in regard to the collateral assignment method, that the Proposed Regulations treat indirect loans to a third party as a series of successive or back-to-back loans the tax treatment of which depends on the relationships of the parties. For example, where an employer (nonowner) advances premiums to an employee's irrevocable life insurance trust (owner), the forgone interest is computed as if the employer made the loans to the employee (taxable as compensation), and the employee then loaned the same amounts to the trust (reportable as gifts).

Controlling shareholder split dollar arrangements.

These particular individuals have an additional problem with avoiding the inclusion of death proceeds in their gross estate through the use of triangular split dollar arrangements. The reason is that while incidents of ownership cannot be attributed to them through the third party they will be attributed to them through the corporation. This is because the insured controls the corporation, and consequently, any incidents of ownership held by the corporation will be attributed to them.

The IRS originally outlined how controlling shareholders might avoid having split dollar death proceeds included in their estates under triangular arrangements through Rev. Ruls. 76-274, 1976-2 CB 278 and 82-145, 1982-2 CB 212. Pursuant to those Rulings, the successful arrangement required that the insured own no interest in the policy and the corporation be relegated to the status of a secured lender. If the endorsement method is applied in accordance with IRS Notice 2002-8 and the Proposed Regulations, the employer must be formally designated as the owner with at least a portion of the policy benefits. Consequently, this approach may not be taken to avoid inclusion of the death proceeds in the controlling shareholder's estate. Alternatively, a controlling shareholder may avoid inclusion of the proceeds in their estate by having a third party structure the transaction as a interest free loan pursuant to the IRC section 7872 regime outlined in the Notice and the Proposed Regulations.

> A controlling shareholder may avoid inclusion of the proceeds in their estate by having a third party structure the transaction as a interest free loan.

Transfer tax treatment of private split dollar.

Pursuant to the Proposed Regulations, in the case of a collateral assignment private split dollar arrangement, if an irrevocable trust is the owner,

84

premium payments made by the donor are treated as loans. If the loan is repayable on the death of the donor, the term of the loan is the donor's life expectancy (tables under Reg 1.72-9) and the value of the gift is the amount of the premium payment less the present value of the donor's right to receive payment. If, however, the donor is treated as the owner under the endorsement method, the donor is treated as making a gift of the economic benefits to the trust when the donor makes premium payments. For example, if the donor or the donor's estate is entitled to receive the greater of premiums paid or the cash value of the contract, the gift is limited to the value of current life insurance protection less any premium payments made by the trustee. On the other hand, if the donor or the donor's estate is entitled to the lesser of the premiums paid or the cash value, the amount of the gift is the value of the current life insurance protection and the trust's share of the annual increase in the cash value less any consideration paid by the trustee.

ERISA Implications of Spit Dollar

Coverage.

Under the Employee Retirement Income Security Act of 1974 or "ERISA," employee welfare benefit plans, which include split dollar plans that are established for employees or their beneficiaries, are subject to the Act's provisions on fiduciary responsibility, reporting, and disclosure. They are, however, wholly exempt from the participation, funding, and vesting requirements. See ERISA sections 201(1); 301(a) (1), 29 USC sections 1051(1), 108(a) (1).

It should be noted that in the case of *Curtis and RJR Circuits, Inc. v. Uncon Central Life Insurance Company,* a federal court held that a split dollar arrangement for a single employee was not covered by ERISA since it did not constitute a plan. Similarly, the Department of Labor issued two advisory opinions during the 1970s which stated that arrangements for a single employee did not constitute a plan under ERISA. Since that time, however, officials from the Department have orally disavowed those holdings. Instead, they have suggested that virtually any arrangement, whether for a single employee or not, is an ERISA plan. In sum, while the Department of Labor can be expected to find that single employee arrangements are ERISA plans, the courts may disagree and distinguish situations involving single employees from those covering employee groups.

Fiduciary responsibility.

The fiduciary responsibility rules under Part 4 of the Act's labor provisions require that a plan be established and maintained pursuant to a written instrument with one or more named fiduciaries that have authority to control or maintain the operation and administration of the plan.

Reporting and disclosure.

The reporting and disclosure requirements are covered by Part 1 of the ERISA labor provisions. There are certain exemptions from those requirements when the plan is for select employees or is small, as follows:

- **Select employees' exemption.** This exemption is outlined in Labor Regulations section 2520.104-24, and applies where the participants are chosen from management or highly compensated employees. In addition, the benefits from such a plan must be paid from the general assets of the employer and/or provided exclusively through insurance contracts or policies (issued by an insurance company qualified to do business in any state) the premiums for which are paid directly by the employer from its general assets. Thus, an employer-pay-all split dollar plan in which the employer pays the entire premium could obtain an exemption under these provisions. If, however, the employee or employee's beneficiary pays any portion of the premium under the plan, this exemption is not available.

> There are certain exemptions from those requirements when the plan is for select employees or is small.

- **Small plans exemption.** The exemption for small plans, which is outlined in Labor Regulation section 2520.124.20, only applies to those split dollar plans that (1) have fewer than 100 participants, (2) for which benefits are paid from the general assets of the employer and/or through insurance contracts or policies paid for buy the employer or the employer and employees, and (3) for which any premium rebates on employee contributions are returned to them within three months of receipt by the employer. Basically, this procedure exempts the plan administrator from the reporting and disclosure requirements except that the administrator must furnish copies of the Summary Plan Description to participants and beneficiaries and provide certain documents to the Secretary of Labor upon request.

Claims procedure.

Under ERISA section 501, a split dollar plan must have a claims procedure. Essentially, this requires that the agreement with the employee must (1) include a provision for written notice of the denial of benefits with an explanation for the denial, and (2) provide a "reasonable opportunity" for a "full and fair" review of the denial by the named fiduciary.

> A split dollar plan must have a claims procedure.

SEC disclosure rules and the Sarbanes-Oxley Act of 2002.

The SEC has finalized rules governing the disclosure of executive compensation for purposes of proxy, registration, and other federal securities law filings. The rules appear to require reporting the Table 2001 or similar amounts for coverage generated by employer premium contributions. Further, if the employee has an interest in the cash value, either the balance of the annual premium or any incremented increase in cash value, payable to the employee on termination of the plan must be reported. These reporting requirements apply to the CEOs of publically traded companies and the four most highly paid executives (where compensation exceeds $100,000) employed at year-end.

As a response to the corporate scandals of Enron and WorldCom, Congress passed and the President signed on July 30, the Sarbanes-Oxley Act of 2002 which requires accounting reforms for public companies. Essentially, the Sarbanes-Oxley Act prevents public companies that are registered under the 1934 Securities Exchange Act from lending to directors and executive officers or their equivalents. This prohibition may apply to split dollar in light of the characterization and required documentation of collateral assignment arrangements as loans by Notices 2001-10, 2002-8, and the Proposed Regulations. It seems less likely that the limitation would apply to endorsement method arrangements. The problem is exacerbated by a lack of clarity in the Act's provision that was designed to leave out existing loan arrangements but which may ensnare future premium advances under a split dollar arrangement. To avoid this risk directors and executive officers or their equivalents under existing arrangements should consider paying the entire premium from their own funds until the law is clarified. The reason is that the penalties for violation of the law are criminal as well as civil. If this presents a financial burden to the participant, the company might consider paying a bonus with or without a gross up for taxes to the participant to cover the cost. In any case, it should be understood that the Act's provisions only apply to public companies and do not apply to nonpublic companies.

Chapter 6

COMBINING SPLIT DOLLAR AND NONQUALIFIED DEFERRED COMPENSATION

The focus of split dollar life insurance arrangements is to provide income tax free and possibly estate tax free death benefits to an employee's family but not retirement benefits to the employee. Conversely, the objective of nonqualified deferred compensation plans is to provide the employee with a retirement income but not tax free death benefits to the employee's family. By combining these two concepts, however, the employee's retirement needs and the family's death benefit protection may be achieved through the use of a single policy with favorable tax consequences.

ERISA Implications

In the case of *Miller v. Heller,* 915 F. Supp. 651 (SDNY 1996), the employer established what appeared to be a collateral assignment split dollar arrangement that provided certain executives with death benefits equal to five times their salaries with the balance of the policies' death benefits payable to the employer. The executives owned the policies subject to the collateral assignments to the employer. The employer paid the premiums and withheld from the employees' wages an amount equal to the value of the term insurance protection payable to the employees' beneficiaries. The employer also entered into a nonqualified deferred compensation plan with the employees to provide a retirement benefit that was equal to 30% of their highest annual salaries plus benefits. In this regard, the employer apparently refused to pay the nonqualified deferred compensation benefits to several employees on the grounds that the benefits were forfeitable and the employees had not met the requirements for vesting. The employees sued for benefits claiming that the arrangement was a funded plan that required vesting under ERISA. The court determined that the nonqualified deferred compensation arrangement was not a funded plan since:

- The split dollar agreement and the nonqualified deferred compensation agreement were separate documents and did not refer to each other in any manner.

- The nonqualified deferred compensation plan clearly stated that the executives had no special rights in any particular assets and only had the rights of an unsecured creditor of the employer. In this regard, the court considered only the written deferred compensation plan document and no other communication to the employees since under New York law oral communications are not considered unless the plan document is ambiguous. It is advisable, however, that great caution be taken to not give employees the impression that they have any rights greater than those of a general creditor, otherwise a court might find that the plan is a funded plan.

> It is advisable that great caution be taken to not give employees the impression that they have any rights greater than those of a general creditor.

Tax considerations.

It should be noted that the court's opinion in the *Miller* case is not clear as to the division of the policies' cash value on the employees' retirement, except to say that the employer was entitled to its share of the cash value. Further, the court's opinion that the plan was "unfunded" represents an interpretation of the term for ERISA labor law purposes and not tax purposes under IRC section 83. The court's opinion is, however, consistent with the two following IRS Private Letter Rulings that plans were unfunded, for tax purposes, where the employers adopted nonqualified deferred compensation and split dollar life insurance plans in combination.

In PLR 6506169720A (June 16, 1965) a nonprofit corporation established, as part of its Participating Physician's Agreement, a voluntary deferred compensation plan under which one-half of each physician's deferrals would be invested in a life insurance policy pursuant to an endorsement method split dollar agreement. The corporation owned the policies and the physicians were entitled to name beneficiaries for the death proceeds in excess of the guaranteed cash surrender values of the policies on their lives. At retirement the physicians were entitled to a sum equal to the cash values of the policies on their lives. Since the physicians were no more than general creditors of the corporation, with regard to their right to the payment of the deferrals, they were not taxable on those amounts until they were actually received. Further, they were taxable annually on the value of the life insurance protection they received at PS 58 rates.

Regarding PLR 8946030, the employer established an irrevocable trust that was to hold and invest funds for several benefit plans including nonqualified deferred compensation and split dollar life insurance arrangements. Since the employees' interests in the trust were nonassignable and subject to the claims of the corporations creditors, the IRS ruled that the employees were not taxable on the deferred compensation until it was actually received.

Overall perspective.

The bottom line seems to be that, from ERISA and tax viewpoints, it is permissible to combine split dollar life insurance and nonqualified deferred compensation under a single policy. This requires that the plan documents are separate and not refer to each other while the employees' rights to the deferred compensation payments are no more than those of a general creditor.

> From ERISA and tax viewpoints, it is permissible to combine split dollar life insurance and nonqualified deferred compensation under a single policy.

Implications of IRS Notice 2002-8 (January 8, 2002) and the Proposed Regulations (July 3, 2002)

As explained in the prior chapter on split dollar, the IRS and Treasury have advised through Notice 2002-8 that they plan to provide comprehensive guidance on the Federal tax treatment of split dollar life insurance arrangements that will be effective for arrangements entered into after the date of publication of final regulations on the subject. Since the Notice also contains a series of safe harbors covering existing split dollar arrangements, anyone already involved in a split dollar/deferred compensation arrangement should review their situation in light of the options provided by the safe harbors. This is especially true with regard to the impact that the forthcoming final regulations may have on the participant's original expectations as to imputed income and the tax treatment of equity cash values.

> Anyone already involved in a split dollar/deferred compensation arrangement should review their situation in light of the options provided by the safe harbors.

For those interested in establishing new split dollar/deferred compensation arrangements, Notice 2002-8 contains significant implications, as described in the previous chapter. In particular, Notice 2002-8 states that taxpayers may rely on it for split dollar life insurance arrangements entered into before the date of publication of final regulations. This seems to mean that the endorsement method will have to be used if tax treatment for the split dollar aspect of the arrangement is desirable under IRC sections 61 and 83. That is because such tax treatment is not expected to be available through the collateral assignment method once the regulations become final since collateral assignment arrangements will be characterized as interest free loans in accordance with IRC section 7872.

The Proposed Regulations that were released on July 3, 2002 continue the economic benefit versus interest free loan regime of Notice 2002-8 but differ from Notice in regard to the taxation of equity cash values that accrue for the employee's benefit. Under Notice 2002-8 such cash values will not be taxed to the employee until rollout, whereas under the Proposed Regulations such cash values are to be taxed annually to the employee.

Plan Diagram

The following diagram shows how a split dollar deferred compensation plan looks:

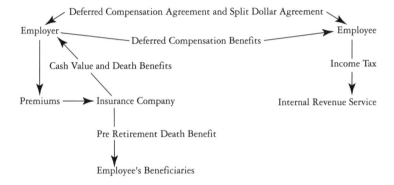

Illustration of Concept

The table on page 90 is how a combined split dollar deferred compensation plan operates. The illustration that may not be used with the public is based on an actual flexible premium variable universal life insurance policy. Assume that the insured is a 50-year-old male non-smoker in the 40% tax bracket and the employer corporation is in the 34% bracket. Further, assume that the initial basic insurance amount is $1,393,154 with a type A fixed death benefit and an annual premium of $26,205. Finally, assume that the hypothetical annual gross rate of return is 8% (Net 6.86).

Year	Age	Annual Premium Outlay ($)	Withdraw ($)	Cash Value ($)	Death Benefit ($)	Split Dollar Death Benefit ($)	Deferred Compensation Benefit ($)
1	50	26,205	0	0	1,393,154	1,000,000	0
2	51	26,205	0	19,346	1,393,154	1,000,000	0
3	52	26,205	0	40,961	1,393,154	1,000,000	0
4	53	26,205	0	63,754	1,393,154	1,000,000	0
5	54	26,205	0	87,775	1,393,154	1,000,000	0
6	55	26,205	0	118,631	1,393,154	1,000,000	0
7	56	26,205	0	151,228	1,393,154	1,000,000	0
8	57	26,205	0	185,689	1,393,154	1,000,000	0
9	58	26,205	0	222,145	1,393,154	1,000,000	0
10	59	26,205	0	262,352	1,393,154	1,000,000	0
11	60	26,205	0	301,925	1,393,154	1,000,000	0
12	61	26,205	0	343,929	1,393,154	1,000,000	0
13	62	26,205	0	388,524	1,393,154	1,000,000	0
14	63	26,205	0	435,943	1,393,154	1,000,000	0
15	64	26,205	0	486,382	1,393,154	1,000,000	0
16	65	0	16,500	495,300	1,376,629	0	25,000
17	66	0	16,500	504,446	1,360,104	0	25,000
18	67	0	16,500	513,363	1,343,579	0	25,000
19	68	0	16,500	522,783	1,327,054	0	25,000
20	69	0	16,500	531,808	1,310,529	0	25,000
21	70	0	16,500	541,107	1,294,004	0	25,000
22	71	0	16,500	550,331	1,277,479	0	25,000
23	72	0	16,500	559,110	1,260,954	0	25,000
24	73	0	16,500	567,831	1,244,449	0	25,000
25	74	0	16,500	576326	1,227,904	0	25,000
26	75	0	16,500	582,311	1,211,379	0	25,000
27	76	0	16,500	587,831	1,194,854	0	25,000
28	77	0	16,500	592,791	1,178,329	0	25,000
29	78	0	16,500	597,018	1,161,804	0	25,000
30	79	0	16,500	600,389	1,145,279	0	25,000
Total		393,075					375,000

Chapter 7

GROUP TERM "CARVE-OUT" PLANS

Design Features

Group term carve-out plans are generally for selected executives and involve replacing their employer provided group term life insurance, in excess of $50,000, with whole life coverage. The protection below $50,000 is kept through the group term plan because it is income tax free under IRC section 79. The coverage above $50,000 is provided through either an IRC section 162 executive bonus plan or a split dollar arrangement.

Regarding group term life insurance under IRC section 79, where the coverage meets certain nondiscrimination requirements, the first $50,000 of protection is income tax free to employees. The value of coverage above $50,000 is taxable income to employees as measured by the Table 1 rates under the regulations to IRC section 79. In addition, the employer is entitled to a deduction for the group term premiums paid.

Short-Comings of Group Term

The problems with group term life insurance include:

• Group plans do not permit the employer to favor executives because of the nondiscrimination rules.

- The coverage is typically reduced at retirement or terminated if the employee leaves.

- Conversion of coverage at retirement or termination of employment is relatively expensive.

- Generally, group term arrangements provide no equity cash values to the executive.

Advantages of Group Term Carve-Out

On the other hand, establishing a group term carve out plan allows the employer to custom design benefits for executives in light of their particular needs. In addition, a carve-out plan offers the following advantages:

> Establishing a group term carve out plan allows the employer to custom design benefits for executives in light of their particular needs.

- The nondiscrimination rules of IRC section 79 do not apply to the carve-out benefits.

- There is no need for IRS approval.

- If the employer takes the split dollar approach there can be cost recovery of the employer's premium outlay for the whole life coverage.

- The executives acquire long term coverage that they can retain after termination or retirement.

- There is the opportunity for executives to obtain ownership of policy cash values with the executive bonus or equity split dollar approaches.

- Under the split dollar approach there may be a reduction in the executives taxable income.

Diagrams of Group Term Carve out Plans

The following are diagrams of the 162 executive bonus and split dollar approaches to group term carve out plans:

Group Term "Carve-Out" Plans

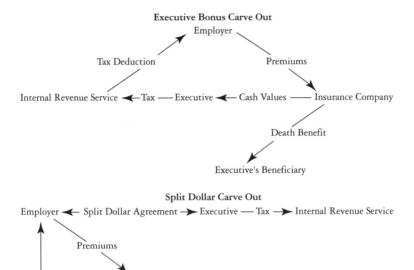

Executive Bonus Carve Out

Employer

Tax Deduction

Premiums

Internal Revenue Service ◄— Tax — Executive ◄— Cash Values — Insurance Company

Death Benefit

Executive's Beneficiary

Split Dollar Carve Out

Employer ◄— Split Dollar Agreement —► Executive — Tax —► Internal Revenue Service

Premiums

Cost Recovery ——— Insurance Company— Death Benefits ——► Executive's Beneficiary

Note about TAM 200002047

In this Technical Advice Memo the IRS ruled that whole life policies that were set up as split dollar insurance, in connection with a group term carve-out plan, should be treated as part of the group term coverage and not as separate split dollar insurance. Consequently, the executives were taxed on the value of the insurance protection under the split dollar coverage at Table 1 group term rates, rather than the insurance company's lower split dollar alternative term rates.

Essentially, the IRS position relied on the finding that the split dollar coverage should be characterized as group term insurance since the whole life policies provided no permanent benefits to the executives. This was because the whole life policies had not reached the cross over point at which the cash values exceeded the employer's premium contributions. Consequently, since there was no equity cash value for the executives' benefit there was deemed to be no permanent benefit that would have precluded the characterization of the split dollar coverage as group term life insurance under IRC section 79.

The IRS conclusion that the lack of equity cash value during the tax years in question meant that there was no permanent benefit seems to be incorrect. This is because it could be argued that the policies did contain permanent benefits for the executives under the equity split dollar arrangements that had been adopted. The cash values had simply not reached the cross over point for the tax periods in question. Further, the executives owned the policies subject to the collateral assignments to the employer. This meant that, while the cash values were subject to the employer's collateral interest, they were still owned by the executives who could have accessed them by paying off the employer's premium advances and terminating the collateral assignments. Finally, application of the IRS finding creates a strange result in that the first year in which equity developed the taxation of the coverage would switch from group term to split dollar.

While not mentioned in the TAM, the employer apparently did not challenge the IRS position since the application of the section 79 Table 1 rates was lower than the PS 58 rates that would have other wise applied once the Service rejected the insurer's alternative term rates. In any case, it seems relatively easy to create split dollar arrangements that are structured to avoid the permanent benefit problem by creating equity for the executives early in the game. For example, the executives might reimburse the employer for a portion of its premiums so that the executives would have an interest in the cash value at all times.

IRS Notice 2002-8 (January 3, 2002) and Proposed Regulations (July 3, 2002)

The Proposed Regulations define split dollar as any arrangement that is "not part of a group term life insurance plan described in section 79." This may be an acknowledgment of the issues raised by TAM 200002047 with a view of avoiding the confusion between split dollar and group term by focusing on the definition of group term under IRC section 79. As indicated by Notice 2002-8, the Proposed Regulations on split dollar eliminate the use of collateral assignment split dollar arrangements like that applied in TAM 200002047. Nonetheless, endorsement method split dollar arrangements are allowed under the Proposed Regulations, which in their final form will presumably provide tax treatment in accordance with IRC sections 61 and 83. This means that the same flaws that existed with the IRS reasoning under TAM 200002047, with respect to the collateral assignment approach, will occur with an endorsement method equity split dollar group term carve out arrangement. Further, since both Notice 2002-8 and the Proposed Regulation state that taxpayers may rely on them until the publication of final regulations, taxpayers interested in creating a split dollar group term carve out may do so utilizing the endorsement method. However, the Proposed Regulations provide for the taxation of equity cash values to the employee on an annual basis instead of at rollout as was provided under Notice 2002-8.

> Taxpayers interested in creating a split dollar group term carve out may do so utilizing the endorsement method.

Illustration of Concept

The table on page 96 is a illustration of a group term carve out plan that uses the executive bonus approach. The actual policy is a flexible premium variable life covering a 45 year-old male nonsmoker in the 31% tax bracket. Assume that premium of $1,751 is paid by the employer corporation that is in the 34% tax bracket. Assume further, that the gross rate of return is 10%. Finally, as previously stated with regard to all the illustrations in this book, this illustration is not to be used with the public.

	Employer			Executive		
Year	After Tax Cost of Executive Bonus ($)	After Tax Cost of Group Term ($)	Change in Cost ($)	Tax Due on Bonus ($)	Cash Value ($)	Death Benefit ($)
1	1,156	238	918	543	0	200,000
2	1,156	238	918	543	0	200,000
3	1,156	238	918	543	0	200,000
4	1,156	238	918	543	398	200,000
5	1,156	238	918	543	1,711	200,000
6	1,156	364	791	543	3,731	200,000
7	1,156	364	791	543	5,873	200,000
8	1,156	364	791	543	8,140	200,000
9	1,156	364	791	543	10,545	200,000
10	1,156	364	791	543	13,091	200,000
11	1,156	681	475	543	15,238	200,000
12	1,156	681	475	543	17,533	200,000
13	1,156	681	475	543	19,976	200,000
14	1,156	681	475	543	22,578	200,000
15	1,156	681	475	543	25,351	200,000
16	1,156	1,045	110	543	28,210	200,000
17	1,156	1,045	110	543	31,260	200,000
18	1,156	1,045	110	543	34,500	200,000
19	1,156	1,045	110	543	37,955	200,000
20	1,156	1,045	110	543	41,642	200,000
	23,115	17,640	11,642	10,857		

Chapter 8

IRC 419A(f)(6) DEATH BENEFIT AND SEVERANCE PAY PLANS

Background

Prior to 1984 employers could prefund severance and death benefits for employees on a tax-deductible basis. Pursuant to the 1984 Tax Act, however, IRC sections 419 and 419A generally eliminate the tax deductible prefunding of those benefits. The reason that Congress made the change was that such arrangements had the advantages of qualified pension plans (tax deductible up front contributions for the employer and income tax deferral for the employees until the benefits were received) with none of the requirements or limitations of qualified plans. An exception to the prefunding limitation was made under IRC section 419A(f)(6) for multiple employer plans involving 10 or more employers where no employer provides more than 10% of the assets of the trust and the arrangement is not experience rated with respect to individual employers. The reason behind permitting the tax deductible prefunding of such plans is that they are supposed to operate like an insurance relationship between an insurance company and an employer.

Tax Pitfalls of IRC Section 419A(f)(6) Death Benefit and Severance Pay Plans

The enactment of IRC section 419A(f)(6), as an exception to the limit on tax deductible prefunding of death and severance benefits, created a rush by some promoters during the 1990s to establish and market such plans involving the use of life insurance as a funding vehicle. Due to the very critical view of such plans that is taken by Congress, the IRS, and the courts, it is advisable to determine how a particular plan stacks up under the requirements of the law before it, and the related life insurance funding, is sold. In that regard, from a tax perspective, there are generally the four following areas of concern:

- **Not separate plans.** The arrangement must not appear on its face to be a 10 or more employer plan when, in reality, it is a plan made up of separate plans for each employer.

- **No experience rating.** The prohibition against experience rating means that for tax deductible prefunding of severance benefits to be allowed, the multiple employer plan must operate like an insurance arrangement in terms of the sharing of risks by the employers that participate in the trust. Specifically, each participating employer must not benefit separately from its employees' forfeitures of benefits. In other words, if an employee looses the right to collect benefits, the contributions that have been made to the trust by that employee's employer must be used to reduce all the participating employers' future contributions to the trust.

- **The plan must not be a disguised plan of deferred compensation.** This means that the plan must only pay benefits on account of the involuntary severance of employment or death of covered employees. In this regard, it is important to review not only the language of the plan but also its performance in operation to make sure that not all covered employees are paid benefits in all events. See *Harvey A. Wellons v. Comm.,* 31 F3rd 569, 94-2 USTC 50402 (7th Cir., 1994). Such a plan should not be established and marketed with the intention of terminating the trust and distributing benefits to all covered employees. The plan should probably not permit participation by controlling shareholders, as it is difficult to imagine how one could have an involuntary separation from a corporation that they control.

> It is important to review not only the language of the plan but also its performance in operation.

- **Deductions under IRC section 162.** The plan should probably not allow the participating employers to completely fund and deduct the contribution for a covered employee's benefit in a single year. This is because it may be too aggressive to take such a deduction in light of the requirement under IRC section 162 that business expenses be "reasonable and necessary" and not prepaid expenses that are not deductible under other sections of the Code. See also IRC section 404.

The Future of IRC 419A(f)(6) Death Benefit and Severance Pay Plans

The IRS through Notice 95-34, 1995-1 CB 309,310 has made it clear that it takes a very critical view of such plans for the previous four reasons. In addition, the Service has "listed" such plans as "Confidential Corporate Tax Shelters" under IRC section 6111(d). This means that participating employers must mention their involvement in such plans on their tax returns. This would seem to be a ticket to an audit and a close examination of the employer's corresponding tax deduction by the IRS. In that regard, the IRS denied deductions and successfully litigated the matter in the Tax court in the case of *Booth v. Comm.,* 108 TC No. 25 (June 17, 1997). The court's denial of the employer's deductions was based on the finding that the plan was experience rated since there was insufficient risk sharing among the employers participating in the Trust. The only risk sharing was with regard to a uspense account that was principally used to pay fees. See also PLR 200127047 in which the IRS determined that the arrangement was a plan of deferred compensation constituting an aggregation of experience rated individual plans which did not qualify under 419A(f)(6).

Besides the IRS's demonstrated hostility to these plans, Congress entertained tax bills in 1999 and 2000 that would have prevented making future tax-deductible contributions to such plans. While those bills were not enacted, they indicate a view among some in Congress that these plans are abusive and should be eliminated. In that regard, bills were also introduced in 2001 (S 1386, HR 2370) that would create standards to control the perceived abuses but allow the inclusion of cash value life insurance in such trusts. Consequently, while the present Republican administration has not shown an inclination to promote legislation to attack these plans their future remains controversial and uncertain.

Most recently, on July 11, 2002, the IRS released Proposed Regulations that are consistent with Notice 95-34 and specifically designed to provide guidance on whether a welfare benefit fund that is part of a 10 or more employer plan meets the requirements of IRC section 419A(f)(6). These Proposed Regulations also mention the listing of 419A(f)(6) plans in connection with the tax shelter disclosure, registration and list maintenance requirements, and refer to the penalties that may apply to those who do not comply. The more salient aspects of the Proposed Regulations are as follows:

- An arrangement satisfies the requirements of IRC section 419A(f)(6) only if the plan is maintained pursuant to a written document that (1) requires the plan administrator to maintain records sufficient for the IRS Commissioner or any participating employer to readily verify the plans compliance with IRC section 419A(f)(6), and (2) provides the Commissioner and each participating employer with the right to inspect and copy all such records. Note that the Proposed Regulation specifically states that a "opinion letter" stating that the plan is described in IRC section 419A(f)(6) does not constitute substantiation.

- A plan must satisfy the requirements of IRC section 419A(f)(6) and the Proposed Regulations in both form and substance. This means that all agreements and understandings (including promotional materials and policy illustrations) will be taken into account in determining compliance with the requirements.

- Generally, a plan is deemed to maintain a prohibited "experience-rating" arrangement with respect to an employer if the employer's cost of coverage for any period is based either on the benefits experience or on the overall experience of that employer or one or more employees of that employer. For this purpose, an employer's "cost of coverage" is the relationship between that employer's contributions (including those of its employees) under the plan and the benefits or other amounts payable under the plan with respect to that employer. This means that the process for determining whether a plan maintains an experience-rating arrangement is to inquire whether the past experience of an individual employer or its employees is used, in whole or in part, to determine the employer's cost of coverage.

- Insurance contracts are treated as assets of the fund. Accordingly, any payments under an arrangement from an employer or its employees directly to an insurance company will be treated as contributions to the fund, and any amounts paid by the insurance company under the arrangement will be treated as paid by the fund. In addition, if whole life insurance policies or similar policies that generate a savings element are purchased under an arrangement, the retained values of those policies reflect the past experience of the employees who participate under the plan. The result is that if such retained values are used to determine the current cost of coverage for that employer (as opposed to being shared among all the employers participating in the plan) the plan will be a prohibited experience-rating arrangement under the proposed Regulations.

Insurance contracts are treated as assets of the fund.

- The proposed regulations list five characteristics that are indications that the plan does not comply with the requirements of IRC section 419A(f)(6) as follows:

The assets of the plan are allocated among the participating employers through a separate accounting of contributions and expenditures for individual employers or otherwise.

Amounts charged under the plan differ among the employers in a manner that is not reflective of differences in risk or rating factors that are commonly taken into account in manual rates used by insurers (such as age, gender, dependents covered, geographic local, or the benefits package).

The plan does not provide for fixed welfare benefits for a fixed coverage period for a fixed price.

The plan charges the participating employers an unreasonable high amount for the coverage risk.

The plan provides for the payment of benefits upon triggering events other than illness, personal injury, or death of an employee or family member, or the employee's involuntary termination of employment.

These Regulations are proposed to be effective for contributions paid or incurred in taxable years of an employer beginning on or after the date of their publication in the Federal Register. Further, for contributions made before that date, the IRS will continue to apply existing law, including the analysis set forth in Notice 95-34 and relevant case law. As to the provisions relating to compliance information and record maintenance for plan administrators, the effective date is proposed to be for taxable years of a welfare benefit fund beginning after the Regulations are published in final form. Existing record retention and record production requirements continue to apply to employers and promoters.

Plan Diagram

A diagram of a section 419A(f)(6) severance and death benefit plan is as follows:

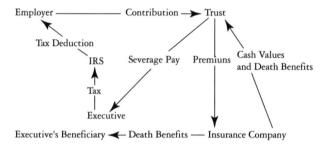

Chapter 9

HOW TO EVALUATE NEW COMPENSATION PLANNING SALES OPPORTUNITIES

The advanced marketing environment produces a constant stream of new ideas involving the sale of life insurance. This requires that life insurance agents and allied professionals determine the consequences of those proposals to their clients and collaterally to themselves. That raises the question of what kinds of issues must be addressed to thoroughly evaluate whether to get involved with such concepts. The purpose of this chapter is to provide guidance on how to deal with new or uncertain tax oriented compensation planning ideas that involve the sale of life insurance. Examples of the types of compensation related marketing concepts that should go through such a due diligence process are:

- Novel applications of well established tax principles to achieve favorable tax results.

- Sales of life insurance or annuity products that address new opportunities in response to changes in the law.

- Combinations of established marketing concepts.

- New uses for existing products.

- Sales of life insurance and annuity products that require coordination with financial instruments and products sold by different entities.

Questions to Be Asked When Evaluating a New Compensation Related Marketing Opportunity

The following are among the questions to be asked when evaluating whether to get involved with a new marketing idea. The list is not suggested to be exhaustive but rather a starting point for the process of examining an opportunity for its merit:

- **What are the professional qualifications of the concept's promoters?** The purpose of this question is to determine the credibility of those you are dealing with. Important information includes their years of experience in the subject as well as professional affiliations, degrees, designations, awards, and so on. Basically, you want to know that they have reason to know what they are doing.

> Determine the credibility of those you are dealing with.

- **What relevant professional licenses do the promoters hold?** This question aims at determining if the promoters of the idea are legally authorized to engage in the business they are after.

- **Do the promoters have E&O coverage?** Should problems related to marketing insurance products in connection with the idea develop, E&O coverage protects the public and may help to shield you.

- **Do suitable products already exist for marketing in connection with the concept?** If specific products are recommended the reasons should be given. The objective is to determine if there are products readily available that may be suitable applied to meet the needs of prospects. This speeds up getting into the market and doing it safely.

- **What financial or other support are the promoters looking for?** The objective is to find out what commitments of resources the proponents may be seeking from you and others.

- **Are there marketing materials available for use in selling life insurance or annuity products in connection with the idea? Do any such materials contain the proper disclosures with respect to any legal/tax and financial risks to sales prospects?** Examples include marketing brochures, seminar materials, and mailing letters.

The focus of this question is to determine the scope of marketing materials needed and whether any existing supplies meet regulatory requirements.

- **Does the concept require ongoing third party administration?** The objective is to determine whether the sale of products must be tied into plan administration and, if so, who is going to do it competently. A major concern is determining that the party assuming administrative responsibility is likely to be around in business for the duration of the plan and that can mean many years.

- **Is the concept already being marketed and, if so, what insurance companies are involved?** The purpose of this question is to find out the level of interest and success that the concept has enjoyed in the marketplace as well as your competitive opportunities.

- **Has an IRS Private Letter Ruling or SEC Take No Action Letter been issued in connection with the concept?** The objective here is to find out if there are any governmental approvals of the concept that affect the degree of legal/tax and other risks that may be assumed by sales prospects.

- **Is a legal opinion available on the concept? If there is, who prepared the opinion and what is the strength of the opinion?** The objective is to assess the strength and credibility of the opinion. In that regard, the following levels of opinions have relevance with respect to Internal Revenue Code penalty provisions 6662 (applying to taxpayers and generally 20% of the underpayment of tax) and 6694 (applying to "preparers" in the amount of $250 increasing to $1,000 where the violation is willful or reckless), Circular 230 (governing practice before the IRS), ABA Formal Opinions 346 Revised and 85-352, and the AICPA Statements on Standards for tax Services. Note, that a "preparer" for purposes of the penalties under IRC section 6694 may include persons who act as mere tax advisors and do not actually fill out a tax return. It should be noted that in TAM 199918060 the IRS rejected the use of an insurer's alternative term rates in a split dollar case and said that it declined to make any conclusions with respect to penalties that might apply to insurance companies and/or insurance agents for supplying incorrect substitute premium rates. The reason the IRS gave for not ruling on the insurer's and/or agent's liability for penalty was that they had not participated in the ruling request. The mere mention of the insurer and agent in this context, however, suggests the possible characterization and liability of such parties as "preparers" in tax cases the IRS has successfully challenged. The easiest way for a taxpayer or preparer to avoid penalty is to show that they relied on the advice of another party. Taxpayers must demonstrate that they made full disclosure to a preparer and the position was taken on that person's advice. Preparers must show that they relied in good faith on the advice of another preparer who they had reason to believe was competent to render such advice. Consequently, if the IRS successfully challenges a new tax oriented compensation planning concept, the strength of any legal opinions issued with respect to the idea may become important in protecting those who had a right to rely on the opinions from various relevant tax penalties. (For a discussion of the percentages appearing next see "Reasonable Basis vs. Other Tax Opinion Standards," Burgess J. Raby and William L. Raby, *Tax Notes,* December 9, 1996, pp. 1209–1212.)

> The easiest way for a taxpayer or preparer to avoid penalty is to show that they relied on the advice of another party.

Nonfrivolous. Applies to protect preparers and represents a 5% to 10% chance of success.

Reasonable basis. Applies to protect taxpayers and represents a 15% to 20% chance of success.

Realistic Possibility of Success. Applies to protect preparers and represents a 33% chance of success.

Substantial Authority. Applies to protect taxpayers and represents a 35% to 40% chance of success.

More Likely Than Not. Applies to protect taxpayers and preparers and represents a more than 50% chance of success.

- *Is a confidentiality agreement required to be signed as a condition of being exposed to the concept?* The developer or promoter of an idea may require that a confidentiality agreement be signed before they will explain the concept. In that regard, the terms of the agreement should be discussed before any substantial disclosure about the concept is made. This is because the idea may not be new or unique and subject to protection under the law as a proprietary interest but signing the agreement may give it that status and bind the user to pay for its application in the market.

Life Insurance Oriented Compensation Plans Summary and Comparison

Type of Plan	Plan Features	Funding Method	Cost Recovery
IRC 162 Executive Bonus Plan	The employer pays for a policy on the employee's life that is owned by the employee.	Permanent cash value insurance.	None
Restricted Bonus	The employer pays for a policy that is owned by the employee but the endorsement limits the employee's access to policy benefits until certain conditions are met.	Permanent cash value insurance.	None
Supplemental Executive Retirement Plan "SERP"	A written agreement to provide the executive supplemental retirement income at the employer's expense through a policy owned by the employer.	Permanent cash value insurance.	Yes
Salary Reduction Deferred Compensation	A written agreement under which the executive deferres compensation to a future time.	Permanent cash value insurance.	Yes
Split Dollar Life Insurance Plan	A written agreement under which the employer and executive share, to varying degrees, the premium cost and policy benefits or structured as a loan to the employee to buy the policy.	Permnent cash value insurance.	Yes

Employer's Tax Deduction	Executive's Tax Consequences	Plan Objective
Bonuses to pay premiums are deducted when made.	Bonuses are taxable income when paid by the employer. Death proceeds are included in the executive's estate if the executive has incidents of ownership.	To provide the executive with a policy they own as a fringe benefit.
Bonuses to pay premiums are deductible when paid unless the employer is considered a beneficiary of the policy, in which case they are deductible when the restriction is lifted.	If the employer is not a beneficiary for purposes of IRC 264 the bonuses are taxable when paid. If the employer is a beneficiary the bonuses are taxable under IRC 83 when the restriction is lifted.	To provide the executive with life insurance as a golden handcuff.
Payments to the executive are deductible when made.	The payments to the executive are taxable when received. Present value of benefits are in the executive's estate.	To provide the executive with a supplemental retirement benefit.
Payments to the executive are deductible when made.	The payments to the executive are taxable when received. Present value of benefits are in the executive's estate.	To enable the executive to defer income, save taxes and accumulate capital.
There is no employer tax deduction.	The executive is taxed annually on the value of the current life insurance protection or the forgone interest. In addition, the executive is taxed on the executive's share of the equity cash value at rollout under Notice 2002-8 or annually under the Proposed Regulations. The death proceeds are included in the Executive's estate if he/she has incidents of ownership.	The purpose is for the employer to provide the the executive financial assistance in acquiring life insurance with cost recovery.

Type of Plan	Plan Features	Funding Method	Cost Recovery
Split Dollar Deferred Comp	Two separate written agreements providing preretirement death benefits and postretirement income benefits utilizing a single life insurance policy.	Permanent cash value insurance.	Yes
IRC 419A(f)(6) Severance and Death Benefit Plan	A multiple employer trust providing severance and death benefits.	Permanent cash value insurance purchased by the trust with employer contributions.	None
Group Term Carve-out	A replacement of group term life insurance above $50,000 with either executive bonus or split dollar.	Permanent cash value insurance.	Not with executive bonus. Yes with split dollar.
IRC Section 457 Plan	Written plan under which employees of State government and tax exempt organizations defer income and earnings thereon to the future.	Permanent cash value insurance.	Yes

Employer's Tax Deduction	Executive's Tax Consequences	Plan Objective
Postretirement payments to the executive are deductible when made.	The value of preretirement life insurance protection and equity cash values are taxable to executive. Post retirement payments are taxable income. Preretirement death proceeds are included in the executive's estate if the executive has incidents of ownership in the insurance. In addition, the present value of post-retirement payments to a beneficiary are included in the executive's estate.	To provide the executive preretirement death benefit protection and post-retirement supplemental retirment income.
Employer deductions are taken when contributions are made to the trust.	The executive is taxed on the current value of life insurance protection. Severance benefits are taxable when received.	Provides the executive with preretirement death benefit and severance pay protection on a tax deductible prefunded basis.
Executive bonus payments are deductible when made.	Executive bonuses are taxable as made. Value of current insurance protection or forgone interest taxable under split dollar.	To provide the executive pre-death benefit protection on a selective basis.
Not Applicable	Payments are taxable when received.	To enable Employees to defer income, save taxes, and accumulate capital.

Glossary

Accumulated earning tax   A tax that applies to corporations' accumulated earnings in excess of certain limitations for the purpose of preventing corporations from being used as a repository to avoid taxation of such earnings in the hands of shareholders. Essentially, it is a tax that is designed to force corporations to pay dividends that will be taxed in the hands of shareholders.

Alternative minimum tax   A tax that is applied to individuals and corporations as an alternative to the regular income tax. It was designed to recapture some of the tax benefits that enable some individuals and corporations to escape significant regular income tax liability because of their ability to take advantage of certain tax benefits. In the case of corporations, annual increases in a life insurance policy's cash value and death proceeds are included in the calculation of the tax.

Alternative term rate   The insurer's term rates that, if meeting certain requirements, may be used in place of Table 2001 for purposes of reporting imputed income for the value of life insurance protection under a split dollar life insurance arrangement.

Constructive receipt doctrine   An income tax doctrine that imposes taxation upon those entitled to income the earlier of when the income is paid or made available.

Economic benefit doctrine   An income tax doctrine that imposes taxation upon the right to the payment of income when the right to payment is susceptible to valuation. This is deemed to occur when the payee is given a security interest in property in connection with the right to payment.

Employee benefit plans   For ERISA purposes, this term includes "employee welfare benefit plans" "pension benefit plans," and plans that are a combination of both.

Employee pension benefit plan   For purposes of ERISA, this is a plan, fund, or program established or maintained by an employer or by an employee organization or by both that provides a pension benefit.

ERISA   The Employee Retirement Income Security Act of 1974 that was enacted as a broad federal statute for the purpose of providing uniform standards for employee benefit plans.

Golden handcuffs   A term used to describe that aspect of a compensation arrangement that is designed to tie the executive to the employer as a method of promoting executive retention.

Income in respect of a decedent   Income owed to a decedent but not payable to the decedent before death. Such amounts are taxed to the decedent's beneficiary with an offsetting income tax deduction for any estate tax attributable to the inclusion of the right to income in the decedent's estate.

Informally funded   A term used to describe an asset acquired and held by an employer for the purpose of paying deferred compensation benefits. The employer is not, however, legally obligated to use the asset to pay the deferred compensation benefits and the asset is subject to the claims of the employer's creditors.

Pension plan   For purposes of ERISA, a plan fund or program that provides retirement income to employees or results in the deferral of income by employees for periods extending to the termination of covered employment or beyond.

PLR   IRS Private Letter Ruling that is issued by the IRS Chief Counsels office and defines the tax treatment of a particular transaction at the request of a taxpayer. A PLR may only be relied on by the taxpayer who requested it but it gives some indication of the IRS position on the issues covered which provides some guidance to other taxpayers.

PS 38 rates   The unofficial term insurance rates provided by the IRS through informal information letters for the purpose of valuing life insurance protection as imputed income under a second-to-die policy used in a split dollar life insurance arrangement.

PS 58 rates   The term insurance rates authorized for use by the IRS in Rev. Rul. 64-328 for purposes of valuing life insurance protection as imputed income under a single life policy used in a split dollar arrangement. Pursuant to IRS Notice 2001-10 the PS 58 rates may be used in 2001 but not thereafter.

Rabbi trust   A trust that is established by an employer to hold assets for the purpose of paying deferred compensation benefits. It provides protection against an employer's change of mind but not against the employer's insolvency.

Rev. Proc.   IRS Revenue Procedure that lays out the conditions for a favorable IRS Private Letter Ruling or "PLR."

Rev. Rul.   IRS Revenue Ruling that is issued by the IRS Chief Counsels office and defines the tax consequences of a particular transaction. A PLR may be relied on by all taxpayers, until it is revoked or modified by the IRS.

Secular trust   A trust established to hold deferred compensation under terms by which the deferred funds are secure from the employer's insolvency. The cost of this protection, however, is that funds going into the trust are taxed to the employee as they are contributed to the trust.

Select group of management or highly compensated employees
A term used to describe a group of employees that are participants in a "Top Hat" plan that is exempt from the more stringent requirements of ERISA.

Substantial risk of forfeiture   Generally, a condition under which the payment of deferred compensation benefits are subject to the participant providing substantial future services as a condition of payment.

Table 2001   The table provided by the IRS in Notice 2001-10 and approved in Notice 2002-8 for purposes of reporting as imputed income, prior to the publication of final regulations, the value of life insurance protection under a split dollar arrangement.

Unforeseeable emergency   Circumstances under which a participant in a nonqualified deferred compensation plan under certain limitations may be paid benefits in advance of the proscribed time without causing the participant to be taxed on the entire amount deferred.

Welfare benefit plan   For purposes of ERISA, a plan, fund, or program whose purpose is to provide its participants or their beneficiaries with certain nonpension benefits through purchase of insurance or otherwise including medical, surgical, hospital, death, accident and disability, unemployment, training programs, day care centers, scholarship funds, prepaid legal services, vacation, severance, and other benefits specified in the Labor management Relations Act.

Resource Guide

Recommended Reading

Protect Your 401(k)

by Chambers, Larry; Ziesenheim, Ken

10 Key Steps you MUST take to protect your—or your client's—retirement nest egg. More important than ever for advisors in today's post-Enron era, and loaded with specific, practical action items you can take to guide 401k's to both growth and capital preservation.

$10.95   Item #T181X-621482

The Long Term Care Planning Guide: Practical Steps for Making Difficult Decisions

by Don Korn

A compact new guide walks you through the maze of issues you need to consider when making long-term care choices. In his simple, straightforward style financial planning expert Don Korn focuses on the most common and crucial factors for determining long-term care needs.

$19.95   Item #T181X-820537

Understanding Erisa: A Compact Guide to the Landmark Act

by Ken Ziesenheim

This new guide clarifies the basic principles of ERISA—and the liabilities to which fiduciaries may be subjected—in simple, understandable terms. Perfect for establishing procedures within your practice, and for ensuring everyone in your organization is in compliance.

$19.95   Item #T181X-48535

Individually Managed Accounts

by Robert Jorgenson

Individually Managed Accounts: An Investor's Guide shows investors what IMAs are, how to use them, and the related pros and cons of investing in them compared to other investment alternatives. The first investor-friendly book on IMAs!

$59.95   Item #T181X-686489

Plan Ahead: Protect Your Estate and Investments

by Frank Eberhart

Written by a professional financial planner, Plan Ahead: Protect Your Estate and Investments will help you get your estate and your financial affairs in order without the expense of a lawyer. Using easy-to-understand language, this comprehensive guide takes you step-by-step through the process of understanding tax and estate laws and creating an estate-management system that effectively addresses your needs.

$16.95   Item #T181X-793683

New Life Insurance Investment Advisor

by Ben Baldwin

The most authoritative resource on today's most dynamic, versatile and adaptable investment vehicle. Term Life, Whole Life, Universal Life, Variable Life and more. Which products are best for you and your clients?? Discover the benefits of each for various client scenarios and life goals—and how to apply them when building solid client portfolios.

$29.95   Item #T181X-41593

These books along with hundreds of others are available at a discount from FP Books. To place an order or find out more, **Call 1-800-511-5667 ext. 183** *or visit our web site at*

www.fpbooks.com
Important Internet Sites

Important Web Sites

- **www.insuranceplanningadvisors.com**

  Halloran Financial Services, specialists in estate and financial planning, providing comprehensive solutions for insurance and long-term care needs for over 20 years. For information contact:

  Halloran Financial Services
  Mike@insuranceplanningadvisors.com
  (781) 449-4556
  400 Hillside Ave, Needham, MA 02494

- **www.financialpro.org**

  For more than 70 years, the Society of Financial Service Professionals—formerly the American Society of CLU & ChFC—has been helping individuals, families, and businesses achieve financial security. Society members can provide consumers expert assistance with: estate, retirement and financial planning; employee benefits; business and compensation planning; and life, health, disability, and long-term care insurance.

- **www.fpanet.org**

  The Financial Planning Association is the membership organization for the financial planning community. FPA has been built around four Core Values—Competence, Integrity, Relationships, and Stewardship. We want as members those who share our Core Values. FPA's primary aim is to be the community that fosters the value of financial planning and advances the financial planning profession.

- **www.fpbooks.com**

  FP Books, a division of SuperBookDeals, is the #1 source for financial planning and investment books, videos, software, and other related products. Find the most thorough selection of new releases and hard to find titles geared towards financial planners and advisors.

- **www.iarfc.org**

  The IARFC is the fastest growing organization in financial services, increasing nearly 3% per month—now over 2,600 professional members. Prospects and clients expect that their financial advisors to maintain meaningful professional standards. There are seven hallmarks: education, examination, ethics, experience, licensing, continued conduct, and continuing education. The RFC designation assures the public an advisor has, and will continue to maintain, the ability to serve in a professional, competent manner.

Publications of Interest

- **E-Alert**
  Thornburg Investment Management
  www.thornburginvestments.com

- **Barron's Online**
  www.barrons.com

- **Kiplinger's Retirement Report**
  www.kiplinger.com/retreport/

- **The Wall Street Journal Online**
  http://online.wsj.com/public/us

TRUST

It s a necessity,
not an indulgence,
in the investor-adviser
relationship.

Clients TRUST their
financial advisers to understand
the real goals that drive them.
But increased competition,
a continuously evolving industry
and unrelenting demands
are making it more difficult
to grow professionally and
guide your clients.

Society of
Financial Service Professionals®

Align yourself with a professional organization that can support your success. The Society of Financial Service Professionals offers:

A choice of nine
Professional Interest Sections

Comprehensive and up-to-date
continuing education

High quality networking opportunities

Client referral, acquisition and
retention tools

Discounts on practice-building
products and services

Society members provide services in the following areas:

- Financial Planning
- Life, Health & Disability Insurance
- Investment Management
- Mutual Funds and Securities
- Retirement Counseling & Planning
- Long-term Care and Eldercare Counseling
- Estate Planning
- Business & Compensation Planning
- Employee Benefits/Group Insurance
- Liability Risk Management
- Tax Planning & Counseling

To learn more call
800-392-6900
or visit
www.financialpro.org

Society of Financial Service Professionals
270 S. Bryn Mawr Avenue
Bryn Mawr, PA 19010-2195

Solutions for a Secure Future™

Free 2 Week Trial Offer for U.S. Residents From Investor's Business Daily:

I NVESTOR'S BUSINESS DAILY will provide you with the facts, figures, and objective news analysis you need to succeed.

Investor's Business Daily is formatted for a quick and concise read to help you make informed and profitable decisions.

This material contains information to help you understand some basic compensation planning concepts involving the use of life insurance products and services that may assist in satisfying your clients' needs. It contains references to concepts that have legal, accounting, or tax implications. It is not intended to help you provide legal, accounting, or tax advice. Your clients should be advised to consult with their own attorneys and/or accountants for advice regarding their particular situations.

About the Author

Louis S. Shuntich is a consultant and author who served in the Law Department of a major life insurance company for 26 years where he specialized in business insurance and estate planning. He received his BS cum laude from Rider University, his J.D. from The College of William and Mary, and his LLM (in Taxation) from New York University.

He is an Assistant Editor of the *Journal of Financial Service Professionals,* a member of the Association for Advanced Life Underwriting Business Insurance and Estate Planning Committee, was Chairman of the American Council of Life Insurance Split Dollar Task Force, and has served on the Life Underwriter Training Council's Content and Techniques Committee. He is a member of the Speakers Bureau of the society of Financial Service Professionals and the Speakers Bureau of the National Association of Estate Planners and Councils. He has also appeared on the CNBC Power Lunch and Health and Lifestyles programs answering questions about retirement and estate planning.